THE MORAL ECONOMY

BOOKS BY RALPH BARTON PERRY
PUBLISHED BY CHARLES SCRIBNER'S SONS

The Moral Economy. 12mo . . *net*, $1.25
The Approach to Philosophy. 12mo *net*, $1.50

THE
MORAL ECONOMY

BY

RALPH BARTON PERRY

Assistant Professor of Philosophy in Harvard University

NEW YORK
CHARLES SCRIBNER'S SONS
1909

170
P464m

COPYRIGHT, 1909, BY
CHARLES SCRIBNER'S SONS

DEDICATED TO N.
MARCH 30, 1909

"Things and actions are what they are, and the consequences of them will be what they will be; why then should we desire to be deceived?"

BISHOP BUTLER.

PREFACE

THIS little book is the preliminary sketch of a system of ethics. Its form differs from that of most contemporary books on the subject because of the omission of the traditional controversies. I have attempted to study morality directly, to derive its conceptions and laws from an analysis of life. I have made this attempt because, in the first place, I believe that theoretical ethics is seriously embarrassed by its present emphasis on the history and criticism of doctrines; by its failure to resort to experience, where without more ado it may solve its problems on their merits. But, in the second place, I hope that by appealing to experience and neglecting scholastic technicalities, I may connect ethical theory with every-day reflection on practical matters. Morality is, without doubt, the most human and urgent of all topics of study; and I should like, if possible, to make it appear so.

The references which I have embodied in the notes are intended to serve the English reader as an introduction to accessible and untechnical literature on the subjects treated in the several chapters. These chapters coincide with the main divisions of ethical inquiry: Goodness, Duty, Virtue, Progress, Culture, and Religion. And although so brief a treatment of so large a programme is impossible without sacrifice of thoroughness, it does provide both a general survey of the field, and a varied application of certain fundamental ideas.

RALPH BARTON PERRY.

CAMBRIDGE, 1909.

TABLE OF CONTENTS

CHAPTER I

	PAGE
MORALITY AS THE ORGANIZATION OF LIFE	1

I. THE GENERAL CLAIMS OF MORALITY . . 1

The practical necessity of morality, 1. The interplay of dogmatism and scepticism, 4. The fundamental character of morality, 7.

II. GOODNESS IN GENERAL 9

The dependence of value on life, 9. Definition of the simpler terms of value. Goodness: the fulfilment of interest, 11. "Good" and "good for," 12.

III. MORAL GOODNESS 13

The moral organization of life, 13. Definition of the terms of moral value. Moral goodness: the fulfilment of an economy of interests, 15. Moral goodness and pleasure, 16. Rightness or virtue, 18. Morality and life, 19.

IV. MORALITY AND NATURE 20

The alleged artificiality of morality, 20. Morality and the struggle for existence, 21. Morality and adaptation, 22. Morality is natural if life is, 24.

V. MORALITY AND CONFLICT 24

Morality and competitive struggle. Morality the condition of strength, 24. The value of conflict, 25. The elimination of conflict, 26. Morality and the love of life, 27.

VI. THE DIGNITY AND LUSTRE OF MORALITY 28

The effect of war on sentiment and the imagination, 28. Real power is constructive, not destructive or repressive, 29. Moral heroism, 31. The saving or provident character of morality, 32. Morality and the consummation of life, 33.

CHAPTER II

THE LOGIC OF THE MORAL APPEAL . . 34

I. THE STAND-POINT OF RATIONALISM AND INDIVIDUALISM 34

Modern individualism, 34. Distinguished from scepticism, 36. The individual as the organ of knowledge, 37. Moral individualism as a protest against convention, 39. Duty as the rational ground of action, 40. Reasonableness a condition of the consciousness of duty, 41.

II. THE LOGIC OF PRUDENCE 43

Prudence as elementary, 43. Interest, action, and goodness, 43. The alleged relativity of goodness, 45. The conflict of interests solved by conciliation, 48. The limits of prudence, 49.

III. THE LOGIC OF PREFERENCE AND PURPOSE 50

The adoption of new interests and the problem of preference, 50. A hypothetical solution of the problem, 51. Solution in the concrete case through the organization of a purpose, 53. The principle of the objective validity of interests, 54. The principle of the quantitative basis of preference, 55.

IV. THE LOGIC OF IMPARTIALITY AND JUSTICE 57

The private interest, 57. The personal factor negligible in counting interests, 58. The refutation of egoism. The first proposition of egoism, 59. The second proposition of egoism, 61. Impartiality as a part of justice, 63. Justice as imputing finality to the individual, 64. The equality of rational beings as organs of truth, 64. Summary of justice, 66.

CONTENTS

V. THE LOGIC OF GOOD-WILL . . . 67

All interests are entitled to consideration, 67. Good-will and the growth of new interests, 67.

VI. DUTY AND THE IMAGINATION . . 69

The logical imagination, 69. Rationalism and incentive to action, 70. Rationalism and faith, 71.

CHAPTER III

THE ORDER OF VIRTUE 72

I. THE VIRTUES AND THEIR CLASSIFICATION 72

Summary of the content and logic of moral value, 72. Virtues as verified rules of life, 73. The material and formal aspects of morality, 74. Materialism and formalism due to exaggeration, 75. The general importance of the conflict between the material and formal motives, 76. Duty identified with the formal motive, 76. Formalism less severely condemned, 77. The five economies of interest, 77. Summary of virtues and vices, 79. Table, 81.

II. THE ECONOMY OF THE SIMPLE INTEREST 82

The simple interest not a moral economy, 82. Satisfaction the root-value, and intelligence the elementary virtue, 82. Incapacity, 83. Overindulgence the first form of materialism, 84. It is due to lack of foresight, 85. Or to the complexity of interests, 86. Overindulgence as the original sin, 86.

III. THE RECIPROCITY OF INTERESTS . 87

Prudence as a principle of organization, 87. Moderation and thrift, 87. Honesty, veracity, and tact of the prudential form, 88. The inherent value of the prudential economy. Individual and social health, 88. Temperance and reason, 90. Prudential formalism, or asceticism, 92. Asceticism illustrated by the Cynics, 92. Prudential materialism or sordidness, 94. Aimlessness or idleness, 94.

CONTENTS

IV. THE INCORPORATION OF INTERESTS. ... 95

Purpose as a principle of organization. Its intellectual character, 95. The virtues subsidiary to purpose, 95. Truthfulness in the purposive economy, 96. The value of achievement, 97. The formalistic error of sentimentalism, 98. Deferred living, 98. Nationalism, 99. Egoism and bigotry as types of materialism. The pride of opinion, 100. Egoism and bigotry involve injustice, 103. The meaning of injustice, 103.

V. THE FRATERNITY OF INTERESTS ... 105

Justice as a principle of organization, 105. Justice conditions rational intercourse, 105. Discussion, freedom, and tolerance, 106. Anarchism and scepticism, 107. *Laissez-faire*, 108. Justice and materialism. Worldliness, 110. Ancient worldliness due to lack of pity, 110. Modern worldliness due to lack of imagination, 111.

VI. THE UNIVERSAL SYSTEM OF INTERESTS ... 112

The economy of good-will, 112. Good-will as the condition of real happiness. Paganism and Christianity, 113. Merely formal good-will is mysticism, 116. Mysticism perverts life by denying this world, 118. Quietism, 119. Mystical perversion of moral truth, 120.

VII. SUMMARY ... 121

The interworking of the formal and the material principles, 121. Importance of the formal principle. Manners and worship, 121.

CHAPTER IV

THE MORAL TEST OF PROGRESS ... 123

I. THE GENERAL THEORY OF PROGRESS 123

The philosophy of history, 123. The meaning of progress, 125. Progress and the quantitative basis of preference, 127. The method of superimposition as a test of progress, 127.

CONTENTS

II. THE EXTERNAL AND INTERNAL PRINCIPLES OF PROGRESS 130

The external principle: the pressure of an unfavorable environment, 130. The external and the internal principle, 131. The internally progressive type of society. The importance of discussion, 132. Rationality the internal principle of progress, 134. The positive motive: constructive reform, 134. Disinterested reflection and the man of affairs, 136. Success depends on moral capacity, 137. The negative motive: revolution, 139. Christianity as a social revolution, 140. The French Revolution, 141. Dependence of progress on the historical connectedness of human life, 143.

III. CONSERVATISM AND RADICALISM . 144

Conservatism values the existing order, 144. Progress requires the maintenance and use of order, 145. The real radical not the sceptic but the rationalist, 145. The justification of the radical, 146.

IV. PROGRESS IN THE INSTITUTION OF GOVERNMENT 147

Institutions are permanent moral necessities, 147. Government as the interest both of the weak and of the strong, 148. The moral necessity of government, 150. The variable and progressive factor in government, 151. The principle of rationality in government, 152. The benefits and cost of government in the ancient military monarchy, 152. Solidarity of interest in the Greek and Roman oligarchies, 154. Advance in liberality in Athenian institutions, 156. The development of modern institutions, 157. The modern idea of democracy, 158. Summary of the modern state. It is territorial and impersonal, 160. The representative method, 160. Emphasis on internal policy and international peace, 162.

V. THE QUALITY OF CONTEMPORARY LIBERALISM 163

Democracy based not on pity but on enlightenment, 163. The respect for the opinion of those most interested, 164. The spirit of modern justice, 165. Sensitiveness to life, 166. The allowance for growth, 167.

CONTENTS

The individual and the crowd, 168. Hopefulness and the bias of maturity, 169. The work done and the work to do, 170.

CHAPTER V

THE MORAL CRITICISM OF FINE ART . . 171

I. THE JUSTIFICATION OF THE MORAL CRITICISM OF ART 171

The higher activities of civilization, 171. The attempt to apply æsthetic standards to life, 172. The claim of art to exemption from moral criticism is based on misapprehension. Morality not a special interest, but the fundamental interest, 174. Morality does not substitute its canons for those of art, 175.

II. DEFINITION OF ART AND THE ÆSTHETIC INTEREST 176

Art as the adaptation of the environment to interest, 176. Industrial art and fine art, 177. The æsthetic interest: the interest in apprehension, 179. The interest in sensation and perception, 181. The emotional interest, 182. Instinct and emotion in the æsthetic experience. Poetry and music, 183. The interest in discernment, 185. The representative element in art exemplified in Greek sculpture, 185. And in Italian painting of the Renaissance, 187. Levels and blendings of the æsthetic interest, 189. The moral criticism of the æsthetic interest, 190.

III. THE SELF-SUFFICIENCY OF THE ÆSTHETIC INTEREST 192

The æsthetic interest is capable of continuous development, 192. And is resourceful, 192. But tends on that account to be narrow and quiescent, 192.

IV. THE PERVASIVENESS OF THE ÆSTHETIC INTEREST 194

The æsthetic interest may supply interest where there is none, or enhance other interests, 194. But it must not be allowed to replace other interests, 195.

CONTENTS

V. THE VICARIOUS FUNCTION OF THE ÆSTHETIC INTEREST 197

Other interests may be represented by the æsthetic interest, 197. The danger of confusing vicarious fulfilment with real fulfilment, 198. And of being æsthetically satisfied with failure, 199.

VI. ART AS A MEANS OF STIMULATING ACTION 201

Art is a source of motor excitation, 201. But such excitation is morally indeterminate, 201. Such influences must be selected with reference to their effect on moral purpose, 202.

VII. ART AS A MEANS OF FIXING IDEAS 203

The higher practical ideas have no other concrete embodiment than art, 203. Art both fixes ideas and arouses sentiment in their behalf, 204. But if art is to serve this end it must be true, 205. Untruth in art, 206. Universality and particularity in art, 207. Art may invest ideas with a fictitious value, 208.

VIII. THE LIBERALITY OF THE ÆSTHETIC INTEREST 209

Art is unworldly, 209. The æsthetic intercourse promotes social intercourse on a high plane, 210.

IX. CONCLUSION 212

When subjected to moral control, art may make the environment harmonious with morality, 212.

CHAPTER VI

THE MORAL JUSTIFICATION OF RELIGION . 214

I. THE DEFINITION OF RELIGION . . 214

The sound practical motive in religion, 214. Religion as belief, 216. Summary definition of religion, 218.

CONTENTS

II. THE TESTS OF RELIGION 218

The measure of religion, extensive and intensive, 218. The test of truth the fundamental test, 220. The therapeutic test, and its confusion of the issue, 222. The two forms of the truth test, cosmological and ethical, 224. The working of these critical principles, 226. Cosmology and ethics are independent of religion, 228. The optimistic bias, 231. Summary of religious development, 231.

III. SUPERSTITION 232

The prudential character of superstition, 232. The ethical idea in primitive religion, 233. The cosmological idea, 234. The method of primitive religion, 235. Superstition in Christianity, 235. The ethical and cosmological correction of superstition, 236.

IV. TUTELARY RELIGION 237

The deity identified with the purpose of the worshipper, 237. The national religion of the Assyrians and Egyptians, 238. The correction of tutelary religion, 239.

V. PHILOSOPHICAL RELIGION. METAPHYSICAL IDEALISM 241

Religion formally enlightened, 241. Metaphysical and moral idealism, 242. The inherent difficulty in metaphysical idealism, 242. The swing from formalism to materialism. Pessimism, other-worldliness, mysticism, panlogism and æsthetic idealism, 243. Æsthetic idealism falsifies experience and discredits moral distinctions, 246.

VI. MORAL IDEALISM 248

Moral idealism reflects moral judgment, 248. Evil real but not deliberately perpetrated. The knowledge of evil, 249. The ground of moral idealism, 252.

VII. THE GENERIC VALUE OF RELIGION . 252

Religion morally inevitable, 252. The value of the religious generalization of life, 253. The immediate reward of service, 254. Religion and moral enthusiasm, 254. Culture and religion, 255.

NOTES 257

INDEX 263

THE MORAL ECONOMY

CHAPTER I

MORALITY AS THE ORGANIZATION OF LIFE

I

IN the words with which this book is inscribed, Bishop Butler conveys with directness and gravity the conviction that morality is neither a mystery nor a convention, but simply an observance of the laws of provident living. "Things and actions are what they are, and the consequences of them will be what they will be: why then should we desire to be deceived?"[1] This appeal, commonplace enough, but confident and true, sounds the note with which through all that follows I shall hope to keep in unison.

It is because he professes to believe that morality is an imposture that must be smuggled into society behind the back of reason, that Nietsche makes a merit of its dulness. "It is desirable," he says, "that as few people as possible should reflect upon morals, and consequently it is *very* desirable that morals should not some day become interesting!"[2] He confesses that he sees no occasion for alarm! But the dulness of morality testifies only to its homeliness and antiquity. For to be moral is simply to be intelligent, to be right-minded and open-minded in the unavoidable business of living. Morality is a collection of formulas and models based solidly on experience of acts and their consequences; it offers the most competent advice as to how to proceed with an enterprise, whether large or small. It is the theory and technique which underlies the art of conduct; that "masterworkman," by whom kings reign and princes decree justice; possessed by the Lord in the beginning of his way, and whom to hate is to love death.

It is worth while to remark and proclaim such a conviction as this only because mankind has so treacherous a memory, and so fatuous a habit of disowning its most precious and dearly won possessions. Cardinal truths are periodically overlaid with sophistication, blended with tentative opinion, and identified with the instruments of the day. There results a confusion of mind that fails to distinguish the essence from the accident, and aims to destroy where there is need to rectify. Because government is clumsy and costly, it is proposed to abolish government; because education is artificial and constraining, society is exhorted to return to the easy course of nature; metaphysics must be swept away, because the

THE ORGANIZATION OF LIFE 3

metaphysics of some time or school has outlived its usefulness; and morality, because it is hard or tiresome, must give way to the freedom and romance of no morality. Such blind and irresponsible agitation is a perpetual menace to the balance of impressionable and unsteady minds, if not indeed to the work of civilization.

Now it is safe to say that these venerable institutions have arisen in answer to fixed needs; needs implied in life as a general and constant situation. There is no other way of accounting for them. They have been tolerated only because they yield a steady return. Their loss would be a catastrophe which mankind, obedient to the necessities of life, would fall at once to repairing. Institutions are the very body of civilization; and while they may grow and change without limit, if they be abruptly destroyed civilization must suffer paralysis in some vital part. At once the most direct and striking proof of this lies in the fact that the revolutionist, whether he be propagandist or man of action, invariably commits himself, and ends by executing the very function he denied. At the moment when he comes to close quarters, and actually engages the object of his attack, he is swept into some current of endeavor that has from the most ancient times been pressing steadily toward the solution of a problem that lies in the centre of the path of life. He straightway commences himself to govern, educate, speculate, or moralize. And the more patiently he labors, the greater his respect for the vested wisdom of his time. Whereas he first sought utterly to demolish, he is now content to make his little difference and hand on the work. In the end every purely destructive programme is inevitably futile, because it goes against the grain. For all conduct is constructive in motive, and forward in direction. But how wasteful is the momentary fury—wasteful of high passion and distinguished capacity, and how mystifying to the lay intelligence!

It may, of course, be said that there is method in this madness; since man's twofold blindness, his dogmatism and his scepticism, his immobility and his wantonness, tend in the long run to neutralize one another. But with the perspective required for such consolation, neither the agencies of destruction nor those of obstruction preserve the same heroic proportions which they are wont to assume in their day. They seem to be engaged in a sort of by-play, and wear an unmistakable aspect of childishness. Lo! Mankind has been a long time on his way, and endures hardily the prospect of endless leagues to go. He is the Patient Plodder, symbol of mature intelligence. And he has in his company two small boys who exhibit an incorrigible naughtiness. The one of these is called Destruction; his other names being Cynic, Sceptic, and Nihilist. He it is that mocks and cries, "Go up, thou bald head! go up, thou bald head!" Mankind does not curse him in the name of the Lord, but invites him to play with another small boy, named Obstruction, and whose other names are Vested Interest, Reactionary, and Pedant. This one, whenever Mankind will lead him, digs in his heels or lies down in his tracks; until, pricked and goaded by his playfellow, he at length gets up and scrambles after. And so these two keep ever by the side or at the heels of Mankind, whom they neither lead nor deflect from his course.

Paradox serves to dislodge prejudice; and blasphemy may rudely but effectually bring to their senses those who have mistaken the hardness of their hearts for loyalty, and their easy default for success. But practical wisdom belongs only to those who proceed unwaveringly out of the past and into the future, correcting mistakes when they may, conserving the good already won, and making new conquests.

It may be remarked, and should be readily granted, that patient plodding is less *piquant* than the by-play of inertia and revolt. The spirit of Nietsche is doubtless even now yawning mightily at such tedious moralizing; fresh proof of the "dull, gloomy seriousness," the hopeless stupidity of our sublunary virtue. I believe that Nietsche has frankly confessed the real grievance of his class of mischief makers. They are impatient and easily bored; while the business of establishing a healthful and vigorous society is complicated, tortuous, and slow. Their talent for letters, their love of vivid pictures, sharp contrasts, and concise dramatic situations, cannot adapt itself to the real bulk and complexity of life. Civilization is too promiscuous, too prolonged and monotonous, for these rare spirits. And they have their sure reward; for they ease the tension of effort, supplying a recreative release from its pangs under the flattering guise of higher truth. All the impatience and playfulness in the world conspires with them. But as one of the demos of moral dullards, I get no little comfort from applying to Nietsche and Ibsen, and to certain prophet litterateurs of England, Burke's reproof of Lord Bolingbroke.

When men find that something can be said in favor of what, on the very proposal, they have thought utterly indefensible, they grow doubtful of their own reason; they are thrown into a sort of pleasing surprise; they run along with the speaker, charmed and captivated to find such a plentiful harvest of reasoning, where all seemed barren and unpromising. . . . There is a sort of gloss upon ingenious falsehoods that dazzles the imagination, but which neither belongs to, nor becomes the sober aspect of truth. . . . In such cases, the writer has a certain fire and

THE ORGANIZATION OF LIFE

alacrity inspired into him by a consciousness, that let it fare how it will with the subject, his ingenuity will be sure of applause.[3]

It is safe to accept morality as one accepts agriculture, navigation, constitutional government, or any other tried solution of an unavoidable problem. There is false opinion here as elsewhere, and hollow convention is not infrequently paraded as duty and wisdom; but the nucleus of morality is verified truth, the precipitate of mankind's prolonged experiment in living.

I do not propose, however, to be satisfied with so modest a claim. It might still be contended that morality is doubtless true so far as it goes, or well enough for those who care for it; but that it will scarcely concern other than the more coarse-grained and less adventurous minds. It is customary to associate high wisdom with the pursuit of some special interest, for its own sake, and under no wider law than a sort of professional etiquette or code of honor. Business is business, art is art, truth is truth, and for one who cares to "go in for it," virtue is for virtue's sake. Those who ride hobbies do not object to the moralist, provided he does not intrude. But if he applies his rules to other than his own personal or domestic affairs, he is berated as an impertinent busybody who is talking of things he does not understand. Now I venture to assert that the moralist in the nature of the case can never be impertinent, though he may be impolite or even insulting. He can never be impertinent because, contrary to the formula of the day, there is no such thing as virtue for virtue's sake. Morality is the one interest that virtually represents all interests. It is the interest of every man in the general tests of success and failure, and in the maintenance of the field or medium of all interests. There is no enterprise which, if conducted efficiently, is not a verification of moral rules; there is no enterprise which does not receive and transmit the flow of life that circulates through the moral system at large. To be righteously indignant is to protest passionately in behalf of the whole good, and against the clumsy and inadvertent evil. To this morality owes its universal support, its invincible finality. It need never be apologetic, because it holds no brief; it advocates no measure except the carrying through to the end of what is virtually undertaken by all parties to the adventure of life.

It follows that no man can exempt himself from moral liability. He is irrevocably committed to life, and can neglect the laws of life only at his absolute or ultimate peril. What does it profit a man to gain a bit here and a bit there, if he is foreordained to loss on the whole? If he squanders his moral patrimony he has no means of recouping his fortunes; he has wasted his supporting vitality and forfeited his general livelihood.

And now if this be true it is of more than passing or sentimental importance. It needs to be vividly realized if morality is to make its saving appeal. Morality is only discredited through being sanctioned; its proper merits are more eloquent than its friends and borrowed auspices. If it can be simply proclaimed as it is, it cannot be denied. This is one of the things which I undertake to do. But to understand what morality really is, to recognize its claims, is to understand also its application, its critical pertinence to art and religion, to all the great and permanent undertakings of men. Such application I shall in the later chapters undertake to suggest, partly as an amplification of the meaning of morality, and partly as a programme of further reflection looking toward a moral philosophy of history. I can do no more in the present chapter than broadly present the structure of morality, leaving the logic of its appeal and its more important applications for the chapters which follow.

II

The moral affair of men, a prolonged and complicated historical enterprise, is thrown into historical relief upon the background of a mechanical cosmos. Nature, as interpreted by the inorganic sciences, presents a spectacle of impassivity. It moves, transforms, and radiates, on every scale and in all its gigantic range of temporal and spatial distance, utterly without loss or gain of value. One cannot rightly attribute to such a world even the property of neglect or brutality. Its indifference is absolute.

Such a world is devoid of value because of the elimination of the bias of life. Where no interest is at stake, changes can make no practical difference; where no claims are made, there can be neither fortune nor calamity, neither comedy nor tragedy. There is no object of applause or resentment, if there be nothing in whose behalf such judgments may be urged.

But with the introduction of life, even the least particle of it, the rudest bit of protoplasm that ever made the venture, nature becomes a new system with a new centre. The organism inherits the earth; the mechanisms of nature become its environment, its resources in the struggle to keep for a time body and soul together. The mark of life is partiality for itself. If anything is to become an object of solicitude, it must first announce itself through acting in its own behalf. With life thus instituted there begins the long struggle of interest against inertia and indifference, that war of which civilization itself is only the latest and most triumphant phase.

Nature being thus enlivened, the simpler terms of value now find a meaning. A living thing must suffer calamities or achieve successes; and since its fortunes are *good* or *bad* in the most elementary sense that can be attached to these conceptions, it is worth our while to consider the matter with some care. An *interest*, or unit of life, is essentially an organization which consistently acts for its own preservation. It deals with its environment in such wise as to keep itself intact and bring itself to maturity; appropriating what it needs, and avoiding or destroying what threatens it with injury. The interest so functions as to supply itself with the means whereby it may continue to exist and function. This is the principle of action which may be generalized from its behavior, and through which it may be distinguished within the context of nature. Now the term *interest* being construed in this sense, we may describe goodness as *fulfilment of interest*. The description will perhaps refer more clearly to human life, if for the term *interest* we substitute the term *desire*. Goodness would then consist in the *satisfaction of desire*. In other words, things are good because desired, not desired because good. To say that one desires things because one needs them, or likes them, or admires them, is redundant; in the end one simply desires certain things, that is, one possesses an interest or desire which they fulfil. There are as many varieties of goodness as there are varieties of interest; and to the variety of interest there is no end.

Strictly speaking, goodness belongs to an interest's actual state of fulfilment. This will consist in an activity, exercised by the interest, but employing the environment. With a slight shift of emphasis, goodness in this absolute sense will attach either to interest in so far as nourished by objects, as in the case of hunger appeased, or to objects in so far as assimilated to interest, as in the case of food consumed. It follows that goodness in a relative sense, in the sense of "good for," will attach to whatever *conduces* to good in the absolute sense; that is, actions and objects, such as agriculture and bread, that lead directly or indirectly to the fulfilment of interest. But "good" and "good for," like their opposites "bad" and "bad for," are never sharply distinguishable, because the imagination anticipates the fortunes of interests, and transforms even remote contingencies into actual victory or defeat.

Through their organization into life, the mechanisms of nature thus take on the generic quality of good and evil. They either serve interests or oppose them; and must be employed and assimilated, or avoided and rejected accord-

THE ORGANIZATION OF LIFE 13

ingly. Events which once indifferently happened are now objects of hope and fear, or integral parts of success and failure.

III

But that organization of life which denotes the presence of morality has not yet been defined. The isolated interest extricates itself from mechanism; and, struggling to maintain itself, does, it is true, divide the world into good and bad, according to its uses. But the moral drama opens only when interest meets interest; when the path of one unit of life is crossed by that of another. Every interest is compelled to recognize other interests, on the one hand as parts of its environment, and on the other hand as partners in the general enterprise of life. Thus there is evolved the *moral* idea, or principle of action, according to which *interest allies itself with interest in order to be free-handed and powerful* against the common hereditary enemy, the heavy inertia and the incessant wear of the cosmos. Through morality a plurality of interests becomes an *economy*, or *community of interests*.

I have thus far described the situation as though it were essentially a social one. But while, historically speaking, it is doubtless always social in one of its aspects, the essence of the matter is as truly represented within the group of interests sustained by a single organism, when these, for example, are united in an individual life-purpose. Morality is that procedure in which several interests, whether they involve one or more physical organisms, are so adjusted as to function as one interest, more massive in its support, and more coherent and united in the common task of fulfilment. Interests morally combined are not destroyed or superseded, as are mechanical forces, by their resultant. The power of the higher interest is due to a summing of incentives emanating from the contributing interests; it can perpetuate itself only through keeping these interests alive. The most spectacular instance of this is government, which functions as one, and yet derives its power from an enormous variety of different interests, which it must foster and conserve as the sources of its own life. In all cases the strength of morality must lie in its liberality and breadth.

Morality is simply the forced choice between suicide and abundant life. When interests war against one another they render the project of life, at best a hard adventure, futile and abortive. I hold it to be of prime importance for the understanding of this matter to observe that from the poorest and crudest beginnings, morality is *the massing of interests against a reluctant cosmos.* Life has been attended with discord and mutual destruction, but this is its failure. The first grumbling truce between savage enemies, the first collective enterprise, the first peaceful community, the first restraint on gluttony for the sake of health, the first suppression of ferocity for the sake of a harder blow struck in cold blood,—these were the first victories of morality. They were moral victories in that they organized life into more comprehensive unities, making it a more formidable thing, and securing a more abundant satisfaction. The fact that life thus combined and weighted, was hurled against life, was the lingering weakness, the deficiency which attends upon all partial attainment. The moral triumph lay in the positive access of strength.

Let us now correct our elementary conceptions of value so that they may apply to moral value. The fulfilment of a simple isolated interest is good, but only *the fulfilment of an organization of interests* is morally good. Such goodness appears in the realization of an individual's systematic purpose or in the well-being of a community. That it virtually implies one ultimate good, the fulfilment of the system of all interests, must necessarily follow; although we cannot at present deal adequately with that conclusion.

The quality of moral goodness, like the quality of goodness in the fundamental sense, lies not in the nature of any class of objects, but in any object or activity whatsoever, in so far as this provides a fulfilment of interest or desire. In the case of moral goodness this fulfilment must embrace a group of interests in which each is limited by the others. Its value lies not only in fulfilment, but also in adjustment and harmony. And this value is independent of the special subject-matter of the interests. Moralists have generally agreed that it is impossible to conceive moral goodness exclusively in terms of any special interest, even such as honor, power, or wealth.[4] There is no interest so rare or so humble that its fulfilment is not morally good, provided that fulfilment forms part of the systematic fulfilment of a group of interests.

But there has persisted from the dawn of ethical theory a misconception concerning the place of *pleasure* in moral goodness. It has been supposed that every interest, whatever its special subject-matter, is an interest in pleasure. Now while a thorough criticism of hedonism would be out of place here, even if it were profitable, a summary consideration of it will throw some light on the truth.[5] Fortunately, the ethical status of pleasure is much clearer than its psychological status. As a moral concern, pleasure is either a *special interest*, in which case it must take its place in the whole economy of life, and submit to principles which adjust it to the rest; or it is *an ele-*

THE ORGANIZATION OF LIFE 17

ment in every interest, in which case it is itself not an interest at all. Now whether it be proper to recognize a special interest in pleasure, it is not necessary here to determine. That this should be generally supposed to be the case is mainly due, I think, to a habit of associating pleasure peculiarly with certain familiar and recurrent bodily interests. At any rate it is clear that the pleasure which constantly *attends* interests is not that *in which the interest is taken.* Interests and desires are qualitatively diverse, and to an extent that is unlimited. The simpler organisms are not interested in pleasure, but in their individual preservation; while man is interested not only in preservation, but in learning, card-playing, loving, fighting, bargaining, and all the innumerable activities that form part of the present complex of life.

Now, it is true that it is agreeable or pleasant to contemplate the fulfilment of an interest; and that such anticipatory gratification in some measure accompanies all endeavor. But there is an absolute difference between such present pleasure and the prospect which evokes it. And it is that prospect or imagined state of fulfilment which is the object of endeavor, the good sought. It is also true that the *fulfilment* of every interest is pleasant. But this means only that the interest is conscious of its fulfilment. In pleasure and pain life records its gains and losses, and is guided to enhance the one or repair the other. Where in the scale of life pleasure and pain begin it is not now possible to say, but it is certain that they are present wherever interests engage in any sort of reciprocity. If one interest is to control or engage another it must be aware of it, and alive to its success or failure. Where life has reached the human stage of complexity, in which interests supervene upon interests, in which every interest is itself an object of interest, the consciousness of good and evil assumes a constantly increasing importance. Life is more watchful of itself, more keenly sensitive to the fortunes of all of its constituent parts. It is proper, therefore, to associate pleasure with goodness; and happiness, or a more constant and pervasive pleasure, with the higher forms of moral goodness. But pleasure and happiness are incidental to goodness; necessary, but not definitive of its general form and structure.

In addition to goodness thus amplified there now enters into life at the moral stage a new element of value, the *rightness* or *virtue* of action which, though moved by some immediate desire, is at the same time controlled by a regard for a higher or more comprehensive interest. This is the distinguishing quality of all that wins moral approval: thrift and temperance; loyalty

THE ORGANIZATION OF LIFE 19

and integrity; justice, unselfishness, and public spirit; humanity and piety. To the further discussion of these several virtues we shall have occasion shortly to return.

Moral procedure, then, differs from life in its more elementary form, through the fact that interests are organized. Morality is only life where this has assumed the form of the forward movement of character, nationality, and humanity. Moral principles define the adjustment of interest to interest, for the saving of each and the strengthening of both against failure and death. Morality is only the method of carrying on the affair of life beyond a certain point of complexity. It is the method of concerted, cumulative living, through which interests are brought from a doubtful condition of being tolerated by the cosmos, to a condition of security and confidence. The spring and motive of morality are therefore absolutely one with those of life. The self-preservative impulse of the simplest organism is the initial bias from which, by a continuous progression in the direction of first intent, have sprung the service of mankind and the love of God.

IV

There is an old and unprofitable quarrel between those who identify, and those who contrast, morality with *nature*. To adjudicate this quarrel, it is necessary to define a point at which nature somehow exceeds herself. Strictly speaking, it is as arbitrary to say that morality, which arose and is immersed in nature, is not natural, as to say that magnetism and electricity are not natural. If nature be defined in terms of the categories of any stage of complexity, all beyond will wear the aspect of a miracle. It would be proper to dismiss the question as only a trivial matter of terminology, did not the discussion of it provide an occasion for alluding to certain confused notions that have obtained wide currency.

Thus there is an ancient belief that it is natural to be licentious; that man is at heart unruly and wilful, wearing the artificial good behavior of civilization as he wears his clothes. Nietsche has contributed not a little to the glorification of this pro-natural and anti-moral monster. And yet no one has recognized more clearly than he, that restraint and law are not only in life from the beginning, but that they are themselves the very sources of its power.

'The singular fact remains,' he says, 'that everything of the nature of freedom, elegance, boldness,

THE ORGANIZATION OF LIFE

dance, and masterly certainty, which exists or has existed, whether it be in thought itself, or in administration, or in speaking and persuading, in art just as in conduct, has only developed by means of the tyranny of such arbitrary law; and in all seriousness, it is not at all improbable that precisely this is "nature" and "natural"—and *not laisser-aller!*' [6]

It only remains to drop the terms "arbitrary" and "tyranny"; since the principle of development in life can scarcely be regarded as arbitrary, or its effectual working as tyranny.

Huxley chose to draw a line between nature and morality, at the point where a limit is set to the isolated organism's struggle against all comers.

> The practice of that which is ethically best—what we call goodness or virtue—involves a course of conduct which, in all respects, is opposed to that which leads to success in the cosmic struggle for existence. In place of ruthless self-assertion it demands self-restraint.[7]

But Huxley appears momentarily to have overlooked the fact that the struggle for existence itself puts a premium on self-restraint. For there is no stage of evolution in which the adjustment and co-operation of interests is not an aid to survival. One does not have to rise higher in the scale of life than the plants fertilized by insects, to observe the working of this principle. It is only the crudest and most impotent self-assertion that is "ruthless." The reason for this is simply that the real enemy of every vital process is not another kindred process, but the mechanical environment. Life is essentially an assertion, not against life, but against death. Interests that expend their energies in destroying or crippling one another, slip back toward that primeval lifelessness from which they emerged. Restraint for the sake of organization is therefore only a developed and intelligent self-assertion.

If one insists still upon drawing a line between cosmical and moral forces, let it be drawn at the point where there first arises that unstable complex called life. Life does in a sense oppose itself to the balance of nature. To hold itself together, it must play at parry and thrust with the very forces which gave it birth. Once having happened, it so acts as to persist. But it should be remarked that this opposition between the careless and rough course of the cosmos, the insidious forces of dissolution, on the one hand, and the self-preserving care of the organism on the other, is present absolutely from the outset of life.

Vegetable and animal organisms do, it is true, adapt themselves to the environment; but their adaptation is essentially a method of using and modifying the environment in their own favor, precisely as is the case with human action.

THE ORGANIZATION OF LIFE 23

Therefore Huxley's sharp distinction between natural plant life and man's artificial garden is misleading.

> 'The tendency of the cosmic process,' he says, 'is to bring about the adjustment of the forms of plant life to the current conditions; the tendency of the horticultural process is the adjustment of the conditions to the needs of the forms of plant life which the gardener desires to raise.'[8]

But this is to ignore the basal fact, which is that plant life in any form is a defiance of current conditions. Art has already begun when natural processes assume a form that feeds itself, reproduces itself, and grows. The first organisms have only a local footing; they are rooted in the soil, and can turn to their advantage only the conditions characteristic of a time and place. Eventually there evolves a more resourceful unit of life, like the gardener with his cultivated plants, who is capable of inhabiting nature at large. But the method is still the same, that of playing off nature against nature; only it is now done on a larger scale, and in a more aggressive and confident spirit. The need of concession to the demands of locality is reduced, through a concession once and for all to the wider processes of nature. But in relation to its environment, life is never wholly constructive, as it is never wholly passive. Whether it appears in the form of vegetation or civilization, it always involves both an adaptation of nature to itself and of itself to nature.

Morality, then, is natural if life is natural; for it is defined by the same essential principles. It is related to life as a later to an earlier phase of one development. The organization of life answers the self-preservative impulse with which life begins; the deliberate fulfilment of a human purpose is only life grown strong enough through organization to conduct a larger and more adventurous enterprise.

V

In the light of this conception let us examine more fully the relation of morality to the competitive struggle between individuals and communities. There can, of course, be no doubt that competition forces life up in the scale. But it is equally true, and more significant, that in the course of that progress competition itself is steadily eliminated. The stronger units of life prevail against the weaker. But the stronger units of life are the more inclusive and harmonious complexes of interest. They are constituted by adjusting interests; allowing each a modicum of free play, or crushing those that will not submit to organization. Within such units the principle of mechanical survival gives way to the principle of moral survival. I mean by this that

THE ORGANIZATION OF LIFE

the selection, rejection, and gradation of interests is made not on the basis of the uncompromising self-assertion of each and the survival of the hardy remnant; but on the basis of the contribution made by each to the life of the collective body. The test of survival is obedience to a law defined in the joint interest of all, and control is vested in the rational capacity to represent this interest and conduct it to a safe and profitable issue. The strength of life thus organized lies in its massiveness, in its effective plenitude. When such units wage war on one another, this strength is wasted; and the very same principle that strength shall prevail, tends to the extension of the organization until it shall embrace contentious factions.

Even where the principle of survival does not operate, conflict has been, and yet remains, a factor in moral progress of enormous and far-reaching importance. The more keen and unrelenting it is, the more effectually does it expose the weakness of the competing units, the more urgently does it require a better concentration and economy of effort. In order to fight a rival, it is necessary to leave off fighting one's self, and be healthy and single-minded. An industrial corporation, in order to overreach its competitors, is compelled to adjust its intricate functions with incredible nicety, to utilize by-products, and even to introduce old-age pensions for the promotion of morale among its employees. And so a nation, to be strong in war, must enjoy peace and justice at home. War has served society by welding great aggregates of interest into compact and effective wholes, the enemy providing an object upon which collective endeavor can unite.

But circumstances that press life forward will be left behind, if these circumstances are not themselves good. And war is not that for which men war; they war for the existence and satisfaction of their interests. That which is constructive and saving in war is not the contact between the warring parties, but their internal coherence and harmony. It is *that* which survives when hostility is inhibited by a recognition of the cost; it is that which is extended when hostility gives way to a wider co-ordination of interests.

The loss when contending currents are redirected and flow together is not a loss of power, but only of neutralizing resistance. It is true that the lesson of harmony is learned through discord; but harmony is none the less in the end exclusive of discord. The principle of peace, learned at home through the hard necessity of war abroad, finds only a more complete justification and beneficent application in peace abroad. It is love and not hate that is the moving spring of life. It is love which is constructive; hate destroys even the very object that evokes and sus-

THE ORGANIZATION OF LIFE

tains it. It is essential, then, to life, not only to assert and reproduce itself, but to increase itself through allying itself with life. Where the motive of life thus freely expresses itself, there are no natural enemies.

I count it to be important thus to trace morality back to the original love of life, since only so is it possible to understand its urgency, and its continuity with every organic impulse. It is because morality is without warrant dislocated from the natural life, that it is accused of being barren and formal. To many minds it is best symbolized by the kindly lady who gives the small boy a penny, and admonishes him not to spend it. But there could be no more outrageous travesty. Morality in its springs is absolutely one with that clinging to life which is the most deep-lying of all interests, and with that relish for life in which its goodness needs no philosopher's approval. The primal determination to be and to sell one's self dearly, is not different, except in its limits, from the moral determination to be and to attain to the uttermost. The whole force of life is behind every moral scruple, and guarantees the sanity even of a universal good-will.

But the identification of morality with the organization of life, serves also to demonstrate life in its unity and larger auspices. Morality harmonizes life and eliminates its wanton self-destruction; but life is not therefore left without an object of conquest. For there is one campaign in which all interests are engaged, and which requires their undivided and aggressive effort. This is the first and last campaign, the war of life upon the routine of the mechanical cosmos and its forces of dissolution. To live, to let live, and to grow in life, constitute an absorbing and passionate task, in which every human heroism may find a proper object.

VI

It must be admitted that the imagination has not yet sufficiently glorified this enterprise of civilization. It is hard to forget old shibboleths and loyalties. And yet precisely that must be done with every advance in liberality. Admiration and passion lag behind reason; are forever backsliding and debauching themselves among the companions of their youth. But man's salvation lies not in degrading his reason to the level of his loyalties, nor in allowing the two to drift apart, but in acquiring a finer loyalty. And while one cannot extemporize the symbols and imagery of devotion, these will surely grow about any sustained purpose.

We hear much in our day of the passing of nobility and enthusiasm with the era of war. "Whatever makes men feel young," says Ches-

THE ORGANIZATION OF LIFE

terton, "is great—a great war or a love story."[9] Love stories will doubtless continue to the end; but must man cease to feel young in the days when cruelty and exploitation are obsolete? Nietsche[10] speaks with passionate regret of a certain "lordliness," or assertion of superiority, that has latterly given place to the slave morality, which aims at "the universal green-meadow happiness of the herd." There are no more heroes, of "lofty spirituality," but only levellers, timid, stupid, mediocre folk, "*sans genie et sans esprit.*"

Now there is a paradox that does not seem to have occurred to Nietsche, in the slave insurrection by which he accounts for this dreary spectacle. It can scarcely be a code of slavishness that has enabled slaves to overthrow their masters. The morality of the modern European democracy is the morality of the strong; of the many, it is true, but of the many united and impassioned, moving toward the general end with good heart. And it is this which gave mastery to the once ruling class. Mastery appears wherever action is bold, united, and with the pressure of interest behind it; mastery has nothing to do with the airs of mastery, with Nietsche's "pathos of distance," separating class from class. The "instinct for rank," and "delight in the nuances of reverence," are not signs of nobility, as Nietsche would have it. There is no nose for them so sensitive and discriminating as that of the chambermaid or butler. The mere pride of an easy mastery over slaves is the taint of every society in which class differences are recognized as fixed. It attaches to all classes; whether it be called snobbery or obsequiousness, it is all one. The virtue of mastery, on the other hand, lies in the power and in the attainment which it represents.

And this Nietsche himself fully admits in his less inspired but more thoughtful utterances. It is "the constant struggle with uniform unfavorable conditions" that fixes the type he admires. When there are no more enemies, "the bond and constraint of the old discipline severs," and a rapid decay sets in; which leads inevitably, after a chaos of individualism, to a period of mediocrity such as the present. In other words, so soon as its political and social activities are confined to "lording it," the aristocracy loses its vigor, and falls an easy prey to democratic or other propagandists *who want something and are united to attain it.*

Now it seems that if man is not to become spiritually bankrupt, he must be confronted with unfavorable conditions that keep him vigilant and alert. Nietsche has no imagination for resistance, struggle, and victory, except as these arise in the war of man against man. His heroes are Alcibiades, Cæsar, and Frederick II, "men predestined for conquering and circumventing others." But it is not easy for us of this day to forget the others; it is the cost to them that galls our conscience. We cannot sincerely applaud a heroism in which life is condemned to feed on itself. Shall the only enemy that never fails, the condition that is always indifferent if not unfavorable, namely, the perpetual wear and drag of nature, be forgotten in order that men may fall on one another? Has man no more lordly task than that of destroying what he holds to be good? Is there no more of "creative plenipotence" in man than killing and robbing?

I am convinced that it needs only enlightenment to reduce Nietsche's circumventer of others to the proportions of a burglar; and to enlarge to truly heroic proportions him who circumvents the blindness of nature, brings up the weak or faint-hearted who lag behind, and throws himself bravely into the enterprise of steady constructive civilization. Nietsche is beguiled by a love of melodrama. He forgets the real war for the pageantry of an era that will pass. As a misleader of youth he conspires with the writers of dime-novels to fix the imagination on false symbols. The small boy who would run away from home for the glory of fighting Indians is deceived; both because there are no longer any Indians to fight, and because there are more glorious battles to be fought at home. War between man and man is an obsolescent form of heroism. There is every reason, therefore, why it should not be glorified as the only occasion capable of evoking the great emotions. The general battle of life, the first and last battle, is still on; and it has that in it of danger and resistance, of comradeship and of triumph, that can stir the blood.

But I have not undertaken to make morality picturesque. I shall leave that to other hands. In an age when it has been somewhat out of literary fashion, Chesterton [11] has found it possible even to proclaim morality as the latest and most enlivening paradox. But I propose to leave it clad in its own sobriety. Its appeal in the last analysis must be to a sense for reality, and to an enlightened practical wisdom. Morality is that which makes man, "naked, shoeless, and defenceless" in body, the master of the kingdom of nature. Morality in this sense has never been more simply and eloquently justified than in the words which Plato puts into the mouth of Protagoras. He first describes the arts with which men contrived barely to sustain themselves, in a condition no better than the beasts which preyed on them in their helplessness. It is then that through the gift of Zeus they are rescued from their degradation and invested with the forms of civilization.

After a while the desire of self-preservation gathered them into cities; but when they were gathered together, having no art of government, they evil-intreated one another, and were again in process of dispersion and destruction. Zeus feared that the entire race would be exterminated, and so he sent Hermes to them, bearing reverence and justice to be the ordering principles of cities and the bonds of friendship and conciliation.[12]

But reverence and justice are more even than the ordering principles of cities. They are the conditions of the maximum of attainment, whether this be conceived as that supreme excellence which Plato divined, or as that all-saving good which is the object of a Christian devotion to humanity. Morality is the law of life, from its bare preservation to its supreme fruition. There is a high pretension in morality which is the necessary consequence of its motive. But man is not, on that account, in need of those reminders of failure which are so easy to offer, and which are so impotently true; he needs rather new symbols of faith, through which his heart may be renewed, and his courage fortified to proceed with an undertaking of which he cannot see the end. Faith and courage have brought him thus far:

> "Till he well-nigh can tame
> Brute mischiefs and control
> Invisible things and turn
> All warring ills to purposes of good."

CHAPTER II

THE LOGIC OF THE MORAL APPEAL

I

There is a phrase, "liberty of conscience," which well expresses the modern conception of moral obligation. It recognizes that duty in the last analysis is imposed upon the individual neither by society nor even by God, but by himself; that there is no authority in moral matters more ultimate than a man's own rational conviction of what is best.

We meet here with the application to morality of the motive which underlies the whole modern reaction against mediævalism, the motive which John Locke so aptly summarized when he said, "We should not judge of things by men's opinions, but of opinions by things."[1] This is individualism of the positive temper, the protest against convention and authority; in behalf, not of license, but of knowledge. Mediævalism is condemned, not for its universalism, but for its arbitrariness and untruth; for its mistaking of the weight of collective opinion, or of institutional prestige, for the weight of evidence.

This is the characteristic temper of the modern

LOGIC OF THE MORAL APPEAL

individualism, whether it be dominated by a bias for sense or a bias for reason. Locke, like his forerunner, Bacon, is an individualist because it is the individual in his detachment from society that alone can be open-eyed and open-minded; who is qualified to carry on that "proper business of the understanding," "to think of everything just as it is in itself." [2] Descartes, although in habit of mind and speculative instinct he has so little in common with the Englishman, nevertheless finds in the individual's self-discipline and concentration the only hope of preserving the savor of the salt of knowledge. Thus he says:

I thought that the sciences contained in books, (such of them at least as are made up of probable reasonings, without demonstrations), composed as they are of the opinions of many different individuals massed together, are farther removed from truth than the simple inferences which a man of good sense using his natural and unprejudiced judgment draws respecting the matters of his experience.[3]

Spinoza, who both abandoned the world and was abandoned by it, sought an individual philosophy of life that should be more universal than the opinion of the world on account of its greater truth. "Further reflection convinced me, that if I could really get to the root of the matter I should be leaving certain evils for a certain good." [4]

This was the impulse in which modern tolerance of individual opinion and appeal to individual conscience originated. It was a protest not against order, but against the disheartening drag, the heavy and dull constraint, of an order externally imposed. Freedom was valued not for the sake of lawlessness, but for the sake of a clearer recognition of the proper laws of things, of the principles that lie in nature and civilization and control them inherently.

Individualism in this sense is not sceptical. Even a charge that existing codes of morality and systems of thought are largely matters of social habit, or rules devised by church and state to maintain an arbitrary and profitable power, does not justify the inference that there is no truth. For there is no dilemma between public tyranny and private caprice. On the contrary, it means that tyranny is itself a form of caprice, and that caprice in any form must give way before reason and experiment. Certain contemporary popular philosophers, such as Wells and Shaw, appear to believe that to repudiate the rigid conventions of the day means to abolish absolute distinctions utterly and fall back upon a general laxity and vagueness. But this is to throw out the baby with the bath. The evil in convention is the substitution of merely *habitual* distinctions for real distinctions, and the only justification for an assault on convention is the bringing of such real distinctions to light.

LOGIC OF THE MORAL APPEAL 37

The individualist virtually claims that an individual's belief, if it be critical, is entitled to precedence over public belief, simply because the individual mind is a better instrument of knowledge than the public mind. It is the individual mind that is more directly confronted with the evidence, more single and responsive. Individualism is not, then, an appeal to private opinion in any disparaging sense. For, in so far as private opinion is independent and truthful in motive, concerning itself with its objects rather than with the social model of the day, it is self-corrective and tends inevitably toward the common truth. It is the opinion that is not really individual, but imitative, respectful of persons, generally submissive to ulterior motives of a social kind, that is private in the bad sense. Its privacy lies in its artificiality, in its partisanship, and in its remove from the open daylight of experience.

If, therefore, one must in moral matters finally rely on the individual's judgment, this in no way implies the breakdown of universal principles. It is neither necessary nor natural that individual judgment should bespeak whim, hasty impulse, or narrow self-interest. The guardian in Plato's *Republic* was as much an individual as the merchant or the soldier.[5] In a sense he was more an individual than these, since he was not swayed by the crowd, but thought with freedom and independence. Nevertheless his thought embraced the interests of the entire community, and comprehended the organization and forms of adjustment through which they all might live and thrive. In moral as in other matters the true appeal of individualism is to an intelligence which, though emancipated from convention, is on that very account committed to the general necessities that lie in the field it seeks to know.

In view of these considerations, then, we may pronounce legitimate and hopeful the moral individualism of the time. It implies the recognition that there is a genuine ground for moral action, which may be brought home to any individual mind that will deal honestly and directly with the facts of life. Morality is not a useful fiction which must be protected against inquisitiveness and cherished in ignorance and servility; it is a body of compelling truth that will convince wherever there is a capacity to observe and reason. It requires no higher sanction than the individual, because the individual is society's organ of truth; because only in the individual mind is society open to rational conviction.

Latitudinarianism and tolerance in this sense bespeak a confidence in morality's ability to justify itself. At the same time they represent a protest against replacing *the intrinsic truth* of morality by the arbitrary standards of authority and convention. Now, while there is little need in the present day of protecting individual judgment against encroachments of authority, there can be no doubt of the great need of protecting it against the more insidious encroachments of convention. This is peculiarly an age of publicity. The forces of suggestion and imitation operate on a scale unparalleled in the history of society. Standards and types readily acquire an almost irresistible prestige, simply through becoming established as models. And the sanction of opinion may be gained for almost any formula, from a fashion in hats to an article in theology. Convention can no longer be accounted conservative. It sanctions promiscuously usages as venerable as civilization itself, and as transient as the fad of the hour. Democratic institutions and universal educational privileges have bred a social mass intelligent and responsive enough to be modish, but lacking in discrimination and criticism.

The tyranny of opinion, the fear of being different, has long since been recognized as a serious hinderance to the development which political freedom and economic opportunity ought properly to stimulate. But the moral blindness to which it gives rise has never, I think, been sufficiently emphasized. We require of business men only that measure of honesty that we conventionally expect in that type of occupation. A politician is proverbially tricky and self-seeking. The artistic temperament would scarcely be recognized if it did not manifest itself in weakness and excess. It is as unreasonable to expect either tunefulness or humor in a musical comedy as to expect a statement of fact in an advertisement. In short, where any human activity is conventionalized, standards are arbitrarily fixed; and critical discernment grows dull if it does not altogether atrophy. It simply does not occur to the great majority of men that any activity should be judged otherwise than by comparing it with the stereotyped average of the day. This is, to be sure, only that blindness of the common mind which Socrates and Plato observed in their day, but it is now aggravated through the greater massiveness and conductivity of modern society.

These considerations will serve both to introduce and to justify my present undertaking. I assume that duty is not an arbitrary mandate which the individual must obey blindly or from motives of fear; but the conviction of moral truth, the enlightened recognition of the good.[6] Hence I wish to demonstrate morality to an individual reflective mind, open to the facts of life and to conviction of truth. I shall expound morality out of no book but experience, "that universal and publick Manuscript, that lies ex-

LOGIC OF THE MORAL APPEAL

pans'd unto the Eyes of all." To refer morality to custom, to conscience in the sense of individual prepossession or institutional authority, even if these be interpreted as the oracles of God, is to justify the suspicion that it is groundless and arbitrary, at best a matter of loyalty or good form. I shall present morality as a set of principles as inherent in conduct, as unmistakably valid there, as is gravitation in the heavens. I shall hope to make it appear that the saving grace of morality is directly operative in life; needing no proof from any adventitious source, because it proves *itself* under observation.

I shall address myself to an individual protagonist whom I shall designate in the second person; and whom I shall suppose to exhibit that yielding reluctance which is the mark of a mind that for very love of truth will not too readily assent.

As I am to prove morality to you, I accept the burden of proof; but you are not on that account totally without responsibility in the matter. As you must not stop your ears, or close your bodily eyes, so you must not shut the eye of the mind, or harden your heart. Were you to adopt such an attitude I should be compelled to set argument aside, and resort to such practical measures as might shock or entice you into reasonableness. Or, I might abandon you as incorrigible. It is clear that I can as little show reasons to a man who will not think them with me, as I can show the road to one who will not look where I point it out. A very large amount of moral exhortation consists in the attempt to overcome apathy and inattention. Such exhortation cannot in the nature of the case be logical, because the subject's logical organ is not as yet functioning. I doubt if there is any discussion of moral matters in common life in which this form of appeal is not present in a measure sufficient to obscure the merits of the question at issue. I desire for present purposes to eliminate as far as possible all conflict and prejudices, and thus to dispense with zeal and eloquence. I shall assume, therefore, that you propose to be reasonable concerning this moral affair. By this I mean simply that you shall directly observe the facts of life, report candidly on these facts, and fully accept the implications of any judgment to which you may commit yourself. I may phrase your pledge of reasonableness thus: "Show what is right, and that it is right, and I will accept it. I mean my action to be good, and ask only to have the good demonstrated to me, that I may intelligently adopt it."

II

It is commonly believed that whereas the logic of *prudence* is unimpeachable, there is a hiatus between this level of morality and those above. To drink one's self to death is a species of folly that the poorest intelligence can understand; but the folly in meanness, injustice, or impiety is a harder matter. Believing as I do that the folly is equally demonstrable in all of these cases, I propose not to accept your ready assent in the simpler case until its grounds have been made as clear and definite as possible. I feel convinced that prudence is not so simple a matter as appears; in fact that it involves the whole ethical dialectic.

I find you, let us say, eating an apple with evident relish; and I ask you why. If you are candid, and free from pedantry, you will doubtless reply that it is because you like to. In this particular connection I can conceive no profounder utterance. But we may obtain a phraseology that will suit our theoretical purposes more conveniently and serve better to fix the matter in our minds. Your eating of the apple is a process that tends within certain limits to continue and restore itself, to supply the actions and objects necessary to its own maintenance. I have proposed that we call such a process an *interest*. In that it is a part of that very complex physical and moral thing called "you," it is *your* interest, and it also has, of course, its special subject-matter, in this case the eating of an apple. It involves specific movements of body, and makes a specific requisition on the environment. Now, still confining ourselves strictly to this interest, we shall doubtless agree to call any phase of it in which it is fulfilled, in which its exercise is fostered and unimpeded, *good*. And we shall doubtless agree to attach the same term, although perhaps in a less direct sense, to that part of the environment which it requires, in this case the apple, and to the subsidiary actions which mediate it, such as the grasping of the apple, or the biting and mastication of it. I mean only that these modes or factors of the interest are *in some sense good;* qualifications and limitations may be adjudicated later.

In this case, which so far as I can see is the simplest possible case of the sort of value that enters into life, the value is supplied by a specific type of process which we may call an interest, and it is supplied thereby absolutely, fundamentally. It makes both this apple and your eating of it good that you should *like to eat it*. If you could explain every action as you explain this action, when it is thus isolated, there would be no moral problem.

We may now safely open the door to the objections that have been pressing for admission.

LOGIC OF THE MORAL APPEAL 45

The first to appear is an old friend among philosophers; but one whose reputation so far exceeds its merits that it must be submitted to vigilant examination. It is objected (I am sure that you have long wanted to say this) that your repast is *good for you, good from your point of view*, but not on that account *really good*. These are the terms with which it is customary to confound any serious judgment of truth; and they acquire a peculiar force here because we seem to have invited their application. We have agreed that your action is good in that it suits your interest, and thus seem to have defined its goodness as relative to you. Now, if we are to avoid a confusion of mind that would terminate our investigation here and now, we must bring to light a latent ambiguity.

We have, it is true, discovered goodness to be a phase of a process called "interest," which is qualified further, through the use of a personal pronoun. The nature of goodness, in other words, is such as to involve certain specific *relations*, here involving a person or subject. Goodness is not peculiar in this respect; for there are very few things in this world that do not involve specific relations. This is the case, for example, with planets, levers, and brothers. There is no planet without its sun, no lever without its fulcrum, no brother who is not somebody's brother.

But the relationship in the case of goodness is supposed to be a more serious matter; sufficiently serious to discredit the meaning of goodness, or make all judgments concerning goodness merely expressions of bias. The supposition is due to the confusion of a relativity in the *subject-matter* of the judgment, with a relativity of the judgment itself to the individual that gives utterance to it. Thus the judgment, "You like apples," deals with your interest and the objects relating to it; but the judgment itself is not therefore biassed. It is no more an expression of your opinion than it is of mine; it is a formulation of what occurs in the field of experience open to all observers. A judgment *concerning* only you, is utterly different from a judgment *representing* only you. The latter, if there were such a thing, would be ungrounded, and would justify the sceptic's suspicions. The confusion is possible here simply because the subject-matter of the judgment in question is itself a judgment. It could scarcely arise in the parallel cases. The lever cannot be defined except in relation to its fulcrum. This may be loosely generalized and made to read: judgments concerning a lever are relative to a fulcrum. It might even be said that a lever is a lever only from the point of view of its own fulcrum. But the most unscrupulous quibbler would scarcely offer this as evidence against the objective validity of our knowledge of levers. Your brother is necessarily related to you; but the proposition defining the relationship is not on that account relative, that is, peculiarly yours or any one else's. Fraternity is a complex involving a personal connection, but is none the less entirely objective. And precisely the same thing is true of goodness. To observe it adequately one must bring into view that complex object called an interest, which may be yours or his or mine; but it will be brought none the less into our common view, and observed as any other object may be observed. Because goodness is inherent in a process involving instincts, desires, or persons, it is not one whit less valid or objective than it would be if it involved the sun or the first law of motion.

Let us now turn to a much more fruitful objection. Suppose it be objected that your action, though good when thus artificially isolated, will in the concrete case have to be considered more broadly before any final judgment can be pronounced on it. To this objection I fully assent. It implies that although we have fully defined a hypothetical case of goodness, we have so far simplified the conditions as to make our conclusions inadequate to moral experience. Accepting this qualification, it is now in order to complicate the situation; but retaining our analysis of the elementary process, and employing terms in the meaning derived therefrom.

Let us suppose that the apple which you enjoy eating, is my apple, and that I delight in keeping it for my own uses. Such being the case, we fall to wrangling over it, and your appetite is like to go unappeased. I now have evidence to show you that your act of violent appropriation does not conduce to your interest. This is simply an experimental and empirical fact. I am in a position to show you that the character of your action is other than you supposed, that you were under a misapprehension as to its goodness. It leads not to the enjoyable activity which interests you, but to a series of bodily exertions and a state of unfulfilled longing in which you have no interest at all. Indeed your action is a hinderance to your interest; in other words, is bad.

But I proceed to point out to you the further fact that, if you will buy the apple and thus conciliate me, you may get rid of my interference and proceed with your activity. Your purchase is now justified in precisely the same manner as your original seizure of the object. If you are asked why you do it, you may still reply, "Because I like apples."

Now, it would accord with the customary use of terms to call such action on your part *prudence;* and prudence is commonly regarded as a virtue

LOGIC OF THE MORAL APPEAL

or moral principle. But in prudence the meaning of morality is as yet only partially realized; it is morality upon a relatively low level. Hence it is desirable to avoid reading too much into it.

On the one hand, prudence does involve the checking of one interest in consequence of the presence of another. You have noted my interest, acknowledged it as having its own claims, and made room for it. Therein your action differs signally from your dealings with your mechanical environment. And it is this contact and adjustment of interests, this practical recognition of the fact that the success of one interest requires that other interests be respected, and dealt with in a special manner appropriate to them as interests, that marks the procedure as moral. On the other hand, while you have acknowledged my interest, you have not *adopted* it. You have concerned yourself with my love of property only in so far as it affected your fondness for apples. In order to appeal to you I have had to appeal to this, as yet your only interest. The moral value of your action lies wholly in its conduciveness to this interest, because it is controlled wholly by it. You are as yet only a complex acting consistently in such wise as to continue an eating of apples. This formula is entirely sufficient as a summary of your conduct, even after you have learned to respect my property. And therein lies its *merely* prudential character. In prudence thus strictly and abstractly regarded, there is no preference, no subordination of motives. Action is controlled by an exclusive and insistent desire, which limits itself only with a view to effectiveness.

III

It would appear, then, that if I am to justify those types of action which are regarded as more completely moral, *I must persuade you to adopt interests that at any given instant do not move you.* I must persuade you to forego your present inclination for the sake of *another;* to judge between interests, and prefer that which on grounds that you cannot reasonably deny is the more valid. In other words, I must define a logical transition from prudence to *preference,* or *moral purpose.*

Let us suppose that, in spite of your liking, apples do not "agree with" you. It is, for example, pertinent to remark that if you eat the apple to-day you cannot go to the play to-morrow. Our parley proceeds as follows:

"Just now I am eating apples. Sufficient unto the day is the evil thereof."

"But you acknowledge your fondness for the theatre."

"Yes, but that doesn't interest me now."

"Nevertheless you recognize the interest in

play-going as a real one, dormant to-day, temporarily eclipsed by another interest, but certain to revive to-morrow?"

"I do."

"And you admit that, apart from the chance of your death in the meantime, a chance so small as to be negligible, an interest to-morrow is as real as an interest to-day?"

"Yes."

"Now, recognizing these two interests, and keeping them firmly in view, observe the consequences of your action if you persist in eating the apple, and pronounce judgment upon it."

"It would seem to be both good and bad; good in its conduciveness to the satisfaction of my present appetite, bad in its preventing my enjoyment of the play."

In your last reply you have fairly stated the problem. You are not permitted to escape the dilemma by simply neglecting the facts, for this would be contrary to the original agreement binding you to be and remain open-minded. And you are now as concerned as I to solve the problem by defining a reorganization of the situation that would permit of an action unequivocally good, that is altogether conducive to the fulfilment of interest.

To understand what would constitute a solution of this moral problem it is important to observe, in the first place, that an action *wholly conducive to both interests* would take precedence of an action which fulfilled the one but sacrificed the other. Were it possible for you to eat the apple now and go to the play to-morrow, your rational course would be to allow your present impulse free play. You would thus be alive to the total situation; your action would in reality be regulated by both interests, or rather by a larger interest embracing and providing for both. An action thus controlled would have a more adequate justification than an action conceived with reference to the one interest exclusively, and merely happening to be favorable to the other interest also. Or suppose that, by substituting a different species of apple for the one first selected, you could avoid disagreeable consequences, and without loss of immediate gratification. In this case you would have corrected your original action and adopted a course that proved itself better, because conducive to the fulfilment of to-morrow's interest as well as to-day's.

We have thus arrived at a very important conception, that of a higher interest possessing a certain priority in its claims. The higher interest as I have defined it is simply the greater interest, and greater in the sense that it exceeds a narrower interest through embracing it and adding to it. Your interest in the fulfilment of to-day's interest *and* to-morrow's, is demonstrably greater than your interest in the fulfilment of either exclusively, because it provides for each and more. In this perfectly definite sense your preference may be justified.

Let us now apply this principle of preference to the more complex case in which there is no available action which will fulfil both interests. Suppose that you cannot both eat apples to-day and go to the play to-morrow. How is one to define a good action in the premises? In the first place the good act originally conceived in terms of the free play of the present impulse is proved to be illusory. There is no good act until your interests are reorganized. In other words, the higher interest, which is entitled to preference, requires some modification of the participating interests. But the higher interest owes its title to its liberality or comprehensiveness. Hence it must represent *the maximum fulfilment of both interests which the conditions allow.* Such a controlling interest may require you altogether to forego the present indulgence, or it may merely require that it be severely limited. In any case, the controlling interest will *represent* both interests, modified, postponed, or suppressed, as is necessary for their maximum joint fulfilment. The higher interest which thus replaces the original interest, and which is entitled to do so only because it incorporates them, I propose to call *moral purpose*.

There are two highly important principles which we have been brought to recognize through this analysis of preference, and it will be worth our while briefly to resume them.

In the first place, no interest is entitled to your exclusive regard merely because it happens at any given time to be moving you. I shall call this the principle of *the objective validity of interests*. I mean simply that an interest is none the less an interest because it does not coincide with an individual's momentary inclination. In reminding you of an interest overlooked, I have not sought to justify it by subsuming it under your present interest. I have not tried to prove that it is to your interest as an epicure that you should go to the play. I have simply pointed out the other interest, and allowed it to stand on its merits. In ethical theories of a certain type, and in much impromptu moralizing, it is assumed that there is no legitimate appeal except in behalf of interests that are at the instant already alive. This is as absurd as to suppose that in order to bring you to the truth in any purely theoretical matter, I must confine myself to evidence that you already recognize. In both cases your individual experience at any given time may be narrow and limited owing to causes that are in the highest

LOGIC OF THE MORAL APPEAL 55

degree arbitrary. It may be advisable that I should solicit your attention by connecting what I have to offer with what is already familiar to you; but this is a psychological expedient. My appeal is logically supported by objects, by principles, by data which are in no wise dependent for their claims on their connection with your present stock in trade.

Chesterton refers to one who "had that rational and deliberate preference which will always to the end trouble the peace of the world, the rational and deliberate preference for a short life and a merry one."[7] I cannot regard such hedonistic opportunism as other than wantonness or wilful carelessness. It may be deliberate in the sense of being consciously persisted in, but I cannot find any rationality in it. It arises naturally enough through the greater vividness of the interests that are already adopted and proved; but all prejudices arise from such accidents, and they are none the less on that account absolutely antagonistic to the rational attitude—that willingness that things should be for me even as they are.

In the second place, it has appeared that there is no demonstrable priority of one simple interest over another differing only qualitatively from it. I propose to call this the principle of *the quantitative basis of preference*. I know that the term quantity has an ugly sound in this context.

But I believe that this is due simply to a false abstraction. Two good books are not better than one because two is better than one, but because in two of a given unit of goodness there is more of goodness than in one. Two is more than one, but not more good, unless that which is counted is itself good. Nor is two longer or heavier than one, unless the units numbered happen to be those of length or weight. To prefer two interests to one does not imply that one is a lover of quantity, but a lover of good; of that which if it be and remain good, the more the better.

At any rate it seems to me a matter of simple candor to admit that "more" is a term implying quantity, whether it be "more room," "more weight," "more goodness," or "more beauty." It seems to me to be equally evident that "more" implies commensurable magnitude; and that commensurability implies the existence of a common unit in the terms compared. Two inches are more than one inch in that they include one inch and also another like unit. Now in moral matters the unit of value is the fulfilment of the simple interest; and in consequence I see no way of demonstrating that one such simple interest is more good than another, as I see no way of demonstrating that one inch is longer than another. But I do see that if I can carry a simple interest over into a compound one, and there both

LOGIC OF THE MORAL APPEAL

retain it and add to it, I shall have more—more by what I add. Such comparison is never a simple matter, perhaps in any concrete case never wholly conclusive. But I can conceive no more important and more clarifying declaration of principle. It means that any rational decision as to the precedence of social ideals, or as to historical progress from good to better, must be based on width of representation and weight of incentive.

IV

If what I have said thus far has proved convincing to you, this may be owing to the fact that you have not been called upon to adopt any interest beyond what are conventionally regarded as your own. In moral matters it is customary to attach a certain finality to personal pronouns. But there are no terms in common use which have so rough and loose a meaning, which cover so equivocal and confused an experience; albeit the necessity and frequency of their use has made them standard currency and polished them into a sort of deceptive smoothness to the touch. There is no term so altogether handy as the term "I," nor is there any so embarrassed when called on to show its credentials in the shape of clear and verifiable experience. If, then, you stand upon *your* interests I shall not be convinced, for I shall not know what you mean. There is no sense in which you are a finished and demonstrable fact. My dealings with you, and this is peculiarly true of my rational dealings with you, cannot be tested by *you* in any absolute or fixed sense, simply because they may *make* you, as they may make me.

Let us return to our test case. You are the epicure, and I am the proprietor; you seize my apple, and I protest. But now I no longer appeal to you merely as one who enjoys eating apples, and warn you that you are selecting the wrong means of attaining that end. I simply inform you that the apple is my property, and that I desire to retain it. I appeal to you to respect my wishes, at least to the extent of non-interference. If you reply that this is no interest that you acknowledge, then I am in a position to inform you. For on no ground can you attach finality to the set of interests which at any given time you choose to acknowledge. If I may remind you of a forgotten interest, I may inform you of a new interest. In the one case, you acknowledge that there is such an interest in that you anticipate its revival, and realize that its mere absence is no proof of its non-existence. You recognize it as having its roots in your organism, and its opportunity for exercise in certain definable and predictable circumstances. This is what you mean when you acknowledge that *you will desire* to go to the play to-morrow. But the evidence of the existence of still another interest, in this case mine, is no less convincing. Like your own latent interest, it does not at the instant move you. But it has the specific character of an interest, and its place in the existent world through its relation to my organism. Recognizing it as an interest, you cannot in the given case fail to observe that it qualifies your action as good or bad, through being affected by it. If your action fulfils your interest and thwarts mine, it is again mixed, both good and bad. In order to define the good act in the premises it is necessary, as in the previous case, to define a purpose which shall embrace both interests and regulate action with a view to their joint fulfilment.

It is customary to argue this principle of impartiality, according to which the merely personal consideration is declared to be irrelevant to the determination of moral value, by a critique of *egoism*. The *reductio ad absurdum* of egoism has recently been formulated by G. E. Moore in as thorough and conclusive a manner as could be desired.[8] That writer analyzes egoism into a series of propositions all of which are equivocal, false, or, so far as true, non-egoistic in their meaning. I shall reduce Moore's propositions to two, and modify them to suit my own conception of goodness.

As an egoist you may, in the first place, affirm that *there are no interests but yours*. This proposition, however, is manifestly false. Accept any definition of an interest or desire that you will, and I can find indefinitely many cases answering your definition and falling outside the class of those which you claim as your own. None of these, if it conforms fully to your definition, is any the less an interest or desire than the one that happens to be moving you at the instant. There would be as good ground for saying that your brother was the only brother, or your book the only book. Even if you abate the rigor of the proposition, you cannot escape its essential falsity. If you affirm that there are no interests but the interests of *each*, or that *each* man's interests are the only interests, you flatly contradict yourself. If you affirm that your interests are of superior importance, that they are exceptional, peculiar, entitled to pre-eminence—this is virtually equivalent to your original proposition. The respect in which your interests seem different from all others either enters into your definition of interest, in which case it becomes general; or it is some adventitious circumstance that does not belong to your interests as such, some accident of proximity which may have psychological or instrumental importance, but cannot rightly affect your judgment of good. For goodness lies in the objective bearing of your action on such things as interests; precisely as the diagonal is a line connecting the vertices of opposite angles in a square, independently of all circumstances that do not affect the generic character of the square.

In the second place, you may affirm that *for you there are no interests but your own.* But this is an equivocal proposition. It may mean that *in your opinion* there are none, in which case you admit the probable falsity of your judgment through contrasting it with the consensus of opinion; through attributing it to your narrowness and false perspective. Your offering it as your opinion gives the proposition at best a tentative form; the question of its truth remains to be adjudicated. I need only present other interests answering your description of an interest to prove you mistaken. And if you were to generalize your proposition and say that each man thinks his own interests the only interests, you would be doubly wrong, in that the generalization would be unwarranted, and the opinion imputed to each man false.

Or, your claim that for you there are no interests but your own, might be taken to mean that in some sense you must confine your endeavors to the fulfilment of your own interests. Otherwise, you may argue, the practical situation would reach a dead-lock, a state of hopeless confusion in which each individual neglected his own proper affairs for the sake of those he had neither the means nor the competence to serve. Now this is indisputably true, but it is not egoism. The judgment that each individual must labor where he may do so most effectively, that he must assume not only a general responsibility for all interests affected by his action, but also a special responsibility for those with whose direct execution he is charged, is an impartial judgment. It expresses a broad and intelligent view of the total situation. In the fable of the fox and the grapes, the action of the fox is due to the folly of a too fluent attention. Similarly, he who lets go his present hold of the web of interests simply because his eye happens to alight on another vantage-point, is as much the blind slave of novelty as the self-centred man is of familiarity. In both cases the fault is one of narrowness of range, of arbitrary exclusion.

Egoists, then, are guilty of a kind of stupid provinciality. They are like those closet-philosophers whom Locke describes.

The truth is, they canton out to themselves a little Goshen in the intellectual world, where light shines and as they conclude, day blesses them; but the rest of that vast expansum they give up to night and darkness, and so avoid coming near it. They have a pretty traffic with known correspondents, in some little creek; within that they confine themselves, and are dexterous managers enough of the wares and products of that corner with which they content themselves, but will not venture out into the great ocean of knowledge, to survey the riches that nature hath stored other parts with, no less genuine, no less solid, no less useful than what has fallen to their lot, in the admired plenty and sufficiency of their own little spot, which to them contains whatsoever is good in the universe.[9]

The impartial or judicial estimate of value is properly recognized as essential to the meaning of *justice*. I do not here refer to justice in the more narrow and familiar sense. Retributive justice, or justice in any of its special legal aspects, is a political rather than an ethical matter.[10] But political justice must be based on ethical justice. And to the definition of this fundamental principle some contribution has now been made. There is a parody of justice, a justice of condescension, that the principles already defined do discredit. For it has sometimes been thought that justice required only a deliberate estimate of interests by those best qualified to judge, as though the settlement of moral issues were a matter of connoisseurship. The viciousness of this conception lies in the fact that qualitatively regarded there is no superiority or inferiority among interests. The relish of caviare is no better, no worse, than the relish of bread. Preference among interests must be based on their difference of representation, or their difference of compatibility. A wide and safe interest is better than a narrow and mischievous interest, better for its liberality. It follows that no interest can be condemned except upon grounds that recognize its claims, and aim so far as possible to provide for it among the rest. No interest can rationally be rejected as having no value, but only as involving too great a cost.

But though these considerations are sufficient to expose moral snobbery, they do not fully define justice. For justice imputes a certain inviolability to the claims of that unit of life which we term loosely a human, personal, moral, free, or rational being. There is some sense in which you are a finality; making it improper for me simply to dispose of you, even if it be my sincere intention to promote thereby the well-being of humanity. You are not merely one interest among the rest, to be counted, adjusted, or suppressed by some court of moral appraisement. I think I may safely assume that there is to-day an established conscience supporting Kant's dictum, "So act as to treat humanity, whether in thine own person or in that of any other, in every case as an end withal, never as means only."[11]

Let me state briefly what appears to me to be the proper basis of this judgment. I have said that I am not entitled simply to suppress your action as may be approved by my own judgment. Now, did I propose to do so, what justification should I offer? I should present, no doubt, the facts in the case. I should show you the incompatibility of your presently adopted course with the general good. But let us suppose that you defend your action on the same grounds. In that case your endorsement of your action has precisely the same formal justification as my condemnation of it. Our equality lies in the fact that we are both claiming candidly to represent the truth. In the last analysis our equality is based on the identity of the objective content to which we appeal. As witnesses of a specific truth within the range of both, the meanest mortal alive and the omniscient intelligence are equal; and simply because the identical truth is as valid in the mouth of one as in the mouth of the other. Where it is a matter of disagreement between you and me, our equality lies in the fact that neither can do more than appeal to the object. Neither has any authority; there *is* no authority in matters of truth, but only evidence. The only rational solution of disagreement is agreement; that is, the coalescence of opinions in the common object to which they refer and toward which they converge. The method of approximating agreement is discussion; which is the attempt of each of two knowers to avail himself of all the organs and instruments of knowledge possessed by the other. Discussion involves mutual respect, in which each party acknowledges the finality of the other as a vehicle of truth. This, I believe, is that moral equality, that dignity and ultimate responsibility attaching to all rational beings alike, without which justice cannot be fulfilled.

Justice, then, embraces these two ideas. In the first place, in estimating the goodness or evil of action, merely personal or party connections must not be admitted in evidence. In the second place, the deliberate judgment of any rationally minded individual is entitled to respect as a source of truth. Conflict must in the last analysis be overcome by the congruence of impartial minds. Hence the justification of reciprocal respect among persons who think honestly; and of a public forum to which all shall have access, and where business shall be transacted under the vigilant eye of him who is most concerned. A candid mind is the last court of jurisdiction. So long as the procedure of society is questioned or resented by one honest conscience, it is lacking in complete verification, and its findings are open to doubt.

V

Enough has already been said to show that the goodness of action must be determined with reference to nothing less than the totality of all affected interests. For this highest principle I have reserved the honored term, *good-will*. Neither you nor I can reasonably decline to consider the bearing of our actions on any interest whatsoever. Right conduct, since it is inconsistent with the least ruthlessness, must inevitably in the end assume the form of humanity and piety.

I know that it is not customary to suppose that devotion to the service of mankind is rational; it is taken to be gratuitous, if not quixotic. But once let it be granted that goodness accrues to action in proportion to its fruitfulness, it follows that that action is most blessed that is dedicated without reservation to the general life. There is only one course which can recommend itself to that fair and open mind to which I conceive myself to be addressing this appeal: namely, so to act in fulfilment of the interest in hand, as either to promote or make room for all other interests.

And this is true not only of such interests as may be assumed to exist, as constitute one's present neighborhood, near and remote; it is also true of interests that are as yet only potentialities, defined by the capacity of living things to grow. If it be unreasonable to neglect the bearing of one's action on interests which one happens not to be familiar with, it is unreasonable to neglect its bearing on interests not yet asserted, wherever there is a presumption that such may come to be. In other words, one's moral account cannot be made up without a provision for entries that have yet to be made. Such a provision will take the form of a purpose to grow, an ardent spirit of liberality, an eagerness for novelty. Good-will builds better than it knows; it is open toward the future; committed to a task which requires foresight and also faith. But such devotion, with all its extravagance, with its very reverence for what is not known but must nevertheless be accounted best, is only, after all, the part of fearless good sense. If anything be good, and if it be reasonable to pursue it, then is the maximum of that thing the *best*, and the pursuit of it *wholly* reasonable.

It may even be said that thrift is only a lesser form of piety, and piety the whole of thrift. For, first and last, goodness lies in the saving and increase of life. The justification of any act lies in its being provident; in its yield of immediate fulfilment and its generous allowance for the other interest, the remote interest, and the interest that is as yet only surmised. The good will is the will to participate productively, permissively, and formally in the total undertaking of life. Only when this intention controls one's decisions can one act without fear of one's own critical reflection.

VI

Let me add a word concerning the part played by the imagination in enforcing the logic of morality. An enlightened conscience, or a rational conviction of duty, will consist essentially in the viewing of life with a certain remove from its local incidents. In conduct, as in all matters where validity or truth is concerned, the critical consciousness must disengage itself and view the course of things in its due proportions, allowing one's dearest interests to lie where they lie among the rest. I have read so admirable a representation of the moral function of the logical imagination in a recent paper by H. G. Lord, that I beg leave to quote it here in full:

As between one's self and another "the image of an impartial outsider who acts as our judge" is none other than this rational insight into the relation existing between two who are cognitively to each other just this and not anything else. It is the vision of the actual reciprocity of the two. From this comes the Golden Rule in its various forms: "Love thy neighbor as thyself," "Do unto others as ye would be done by," "Put yourself in his place." But, furthermore, even this simpler justice necessitates the power not only to "see yourself as others see you," but even more adequately, and as we say more justly, to put yourself where you belong in a system of many, in which you not only count for one and no more than one, but in which you count for just that sort of one, fulfilling just that sort of function which your place in the rationally conceived system involves or necessitates. And this gives us a form of justice much more profound and complex than that of the Golden Rule, and requiring constructive imagination and rational insight of the very highest order. And with this insight goes necessarily an inevitableness, an inexorableness, and, as we say metaphorically, an imperativeness, which no amount of twisting and intellectual thimble-rigging can avoid. The logic of the system cannot be avoided any more than a step in a mathematical demonstration. . . . So long as it stands, its parts, elements, or members are *placed*, and there is set over each of them the imperative of the system in which they are members.[12]

It has sometimes been thought that a fair view of life will inhibit action through discrediting party zeal. John Davidson describes what he calls "the apathy of intelligence."

To be strong to the end, it is necessary to shut many windows, to be deaf on either side of the head at will, to fetter the mind. . . . The perfect intelligence cannot fight, cannot compete. Intelligence, fully awake, is doomed to understand, and can no more take part in the disputes of men than in the disputes of other male creatures.[13]

Now it is true that intelligence inhibits wantonness; for intelligence, fully awake, knows how unreasonable it is that one who loves life should

LOGIC OF THE MORAL APPEAL

destroy it. But because intelligence affirms the motive of each combatant, it must move action to the saving of both. Where intelligence is directed to the inner impulse of life, it is not apathetic, but sympathetic. Its span is widened, while its incentive is not divided but multiplied.

Nor does it follow that when duty is interpreted as enlightenment, life must lose its romantic flavor and cease to require the old high-spirited virtues. It is this very linking of life to life, this abandonment of one's self to the prodigious of the whole, that provides the true object of reverence, and permits the sense of mystery to remain even after the light has come. Although the way of morality is evident and well-proved in direction, being plain to whomever will look at life with a fair and commanding eye, achievement is difficult, the great victories hard won, and the certain prospect bounded by a near horizon. Even though life be rationalized, it will none the less call for intrepid faith; for what Maeterlinck calls "the heroic, cloud-tipped, indefatigable energy of our conscience." [14]

CHAPTER III

THE ORDER OF VIRTUE

I

We have thus far dealt with the general content of morality, and with its logical grounds. Morality is only life where life is organized and confident, the struggle for mere existence being replaced with the prospect of a progressive and limitless attainment. The good is fulfilled desire; the moral good the fulfilment of a universal economy, embracing all desires, actual and possible, and providing for them as liberally as their mutual relations permit. The moral good is simply the greatest possible good, where good in the broad generic sense means any object of interest whatsoever, anything proved worth the seeking from the fact that some unit of life actually seeks it. Whatever is prized is on that account precious.

The logic of morality rests on this objective relation between interest and value. The maximum good has the greatest weight, its claims are entitled to priority, because it surpasses any limited good in incentive and promise of fulfilment. Duty in this logical sense is simply the

THE ORDER OF VIRTUE

control of particular actions by a full recognition of their consequences.

In the present chapter the attention is shifted from the whole to the parts of morality. I am not one of those who stake much on the casuistical application of ethical principles. Every particular action virtually involves considerations of enormous complexity; and the individual must be mainly guided by general rules of conduct or *virtues*, which are proved by the cumulative experience of the race. Life itself is the only adequate experiment in living. Virtues are properly verified only in the history of society, in the development of institutions, and in the evidences of progress in civilization at large. I shall confine myself, then, to such verified virtues, and seek to show their relation to morality as a whole.[1]

Virtues vary in generality according to the degree to which they refer to special circumstance; and, since there is no limit to the variety of circumstance, there is, strictly speaking, no final and comprehensive order of virtues. The term may be applied with equal propriety to types of action as universal as justice and as particular as conjugal fidelity. We shall find it necessary to confine ourselves to the more general and fundamental virtues.

I have adopted a method of classification to which I attach no absolute importance, but which will, I trust, serve to amplify and illuminate the fundamental conceptions which I have already formulated. I shall aim, in the first place, to make explicit a distinction which has hitherto been obscured. I refer to the difference between the *material* and the *formal* aspects of morality. On the one hand, action is always engaged in the fulfilment of an immediate interest; this constitutes its material goodness. On the other hand, every moral action is limited or regulated by the provision which it makes for ulterior interests; this constitutes its formal goodness. Let me make this difference more clear.

A particular action is invariably connected with a particular interest; and in so far as it is successful it will thus be directly fruitful of fulfilment. And it matters not how broad a purpose constitutes its ultimate motive; for purposes can be served only through a variety of activities, each of which will have its proximate interest and its own continuous yield of satisfaction. Life pays as it goes, even though it goes to the length of serving humanity at large, and the larger enterprises owe their very justification to this additive and cumulative principle.

But if action is to be moral it must always look beyond the present satisfaction. It must submit to such checks as are necessary for the realization of a greater good. Indeed, action is not wholly

THE ORDER OF VIRTUE

good until it is controlled with reference to the fulfilment of the totality of interests.

It follows, then, that every action may be judged in two respects: first, in respect of its immediate return of fulfilment; second, in respect of its bearing on all residual interests. Every good action will be both profitable and safe; both self-sustaining and also serviceable to the whole.

The necessity of determining the relative weight which is to be given to these two considerations accounts for the peculiar delicacy of the art of life, since it makes almost inevitable either the one or the other of two opposite errors of exaggeration. The *undue assertion of the present interest* constitutes materialism, in the moral sense. Materialism is a forfeiture of greater good through preoccupation with nearer good. It appears in an individual's neglect of his fellow's interest, in his too easy satisfaction with good already attained, in short-sighted policy on any scale. Formalism, on the other hand, signifies the *improvident exaggeration of ulterior motives*. It is due to a misapprehension concerning the relation between higher and lower interests. I have sought to make it clear that higher interests owe their eminence, not to any intrinsic quality of their own, but to the fact that they save and promote lower interests. Formalism is the rejection of lower interests in the name of some good that without these interests is nothing.

The conflict between the material and formal motives in life is present in every moral crisis, and qualifies the meaning of every moral idea. It may even provoke a social revolution, as in the case of the Puritan revolution in England. The Puritan is still the symbol of moral rigor and sobriety, as the Cavalier is the symbol of the love of life. The full meaning of morality tends constantly to be confused through identifying it exclusively with the one or the other of these motives. Thus morality has come, on the whole, to be associated with constraint and discipline, in both a favorable and a disparaging sense. This has led to its being rejected as a falsification of life by those who insist that every good thing is free and fair and pleasant. And, even among those who recognize the vital necessity of discipline, morality is so narrowed to that component, that it commonly suggests only those scruples and inhibitions which destroy the spontaneity and whole-heartedness of every activity.

That morality should tend to be identified with its formal rather than its material aspect is not strange; for it is the formal motive which is critical and corrective, substituting a conscious reconstruction of interests for their initial movement. It is this fact which gives to duty that

THE ORDER OF VIRTUE

sense of compulsion which is so invariably associated with it. Duty is opposed to the line of least resistance, whenever life is dominated by any motive short of the absolute good-will. Thus among the Greeks, δίκη is opposed to βία.[2] This means simply that because the principles of social organization are not as yet thoroughly assimilated, their adoption requires attention and effort. And a similar opposition may appear at either a higher or lower level, between the momentary impulse and the law of prudence, or between the habit of worldliness and the law of piety.

In connection with this broad difference between the material and formal aspects of life, it is interesting to observe a certain difference of leniency in the popular judgment. Materialism is more heartily condemned, because he who is guilty of it is not alive to the general good. He is morally unregenerate. Formalism, on the other hand, is good-hearted or well-intentioned. He who is guilty of it may be ridiculed as unpractical, or pitied for his misguided zeal; but society rarely offers to chastise him. For he has submitted to discipline, and if he is not the friend of man, it is not because of any profit that he has reserved for himself.

In the arrangement which follows I shall use this difference between the material and formal aspects of morality to supplement the main principle of classification, which is that difference of level or range, of which I have already made some use in the previous chapter, and which I shall now define more precisely. In morality life is so organized as to provide for interests as liberally and comprehensively as possible. But the principles through which such organization is effected will differ in the degree to which they accomplish that end. Hence it is possible to define several economies or stages of organization which are successively more complete. The *simple interest*, first, is the isolated interest, pursued regardlessly of other interests; in other words, not as yet brought under the form of morality. The *reciprocity of interests*, represents that rudimentary form of morality in which interests enter only into an external relation, through which they secure an exchange of benefits without abandoning their independence. In the *incorporation of interests*, elementary interests are unified through a purpose which subordinates and regulates them. The *fraternity of interests*, is that organization in which the rational or personal unit of interest is recognized as final, and respected wherever it is met. But there must also be some last economy, in which provision is formally made for any interest whatsoever that may assert itself. This is the realm of

THE ORDER OF VIRTUE

good-will, or, as I shall call it for the sake of symmetry, the *universal system of interests*. I shall so construe these economies as to make the broader or more inclusive comprehend the narrower.

Now each of these economies possesses its characteristic principle of organization, or typical mode of action; and this enables us to define five prime virtues: *intelligence, prudence, purpose, justice,* and *good-will.* From each of these virtues there accrues to life a characteristic benefit: from intelligence, *satisfaction;* from prudence, *health;* from purpose, *achievement;* from justice, *rational intercourse;* and from good-will, *religion.* The absence of these virtues defines a group of negative vices: *incapacity, imprudence, aimlessness, injustice,* and *irreverence.* Finally, applying the distinction between formalism and materialism, we obtain two further series of vices; for, with two exceptions, it is possible in each economy either to exaggerate the principle of organization, and thus neglect the constituent interests which it is intended to organize; or to exaggerate the good attained, and thus neglect the wider spheres beyond. There will thus be a formalistic series of errors: *asceticism, sentimentalism, anarchism, mysticism;* and a materialistic series: *overindulgence, sordidness, bigotry* or *egoism, worldliness.* Since materialism is in each case due to the lack of the next higher principle of organization, there is no real difference between the materialism of one economy and the negative vice of the next. But I have thought it worth while to retain both series, because they represent a difference of emphasis which it is customary to make. Thus there is no real difference between overindulgence and imprudence; but one refers to the excess, and the other to the deficiency, in an activity which is excessive in its fulfilment of a present interest, and deficient in its regard for ulterior interests.

I have thought it best for the purpose of clear presentation to tabulate these virtues and vices; and it proves convenient, also, to adopt a fixed nomenclature. It is unfortunate that the terms must be drawn from common speech; for it is impossible that the meaning assigned to them in the course of a methodical analysis like the present, should exactly coincide with that which they have acquired in their looser application to daily life. But I shall endeavor always to make plain the sense in which I use them; and, thus guarded, they will serve to mark out a series of special topics which it is important briefly to review.

THE ORDER OF VIRTUE

ECONOMY	VIRTUE	VALUE	NEGATIVE VICE	FORMALISM	MATERIALISM
Simple Interest	Intelligence	Satisfaction	Incapacity	—	Overindulgence
Reciprocity of Interests	Prudence	Health	Imprudence	Asceticism	Sordidness
Incorporation of Interests	Purpose	Achievement	Aimlessness	Sentimentalism	Bigotry Egoism
Fraternity of Interests	Justice	Rational Intercourse	Injustice	Anarchism	Worldliness
Universal System of Interests	Good-Will	Religion	Irreverence	Mysticism	—

II

We have already had occasion to remark that no *moral* value attaches to the successes and failures of the isolated or *simple interest*. Thus it is customary not to apply judgments of approval or condemnation to the vicissitudes of animal life. So wholesale a generalization is undoubtedly false; but at any rate it is based on the supposition that the motive in animal life is always simple. And similarly, whenever human action is regarded only with reference to the impulse it immediately serves, it is judged to be successful or futile, but never right or wrong. These properties are reserved for such action as is controlled, or is capable of being controlled, with reference both to an immediate and also an ulterior interest. But since the difference between goodness in the wider generic sense and goodness in the moral sense is one of complexity, it is proper and illuminating to bring them into one orderly progression.

The *root-value*, then, of which all the higher moral values are compounded, is the fulfilment or satisfaction of the particular interest. This fundamental value is conditioned by a form of organization, which I propose in a restricted sense to term *intelligence*. I mean the capacity which every living interest must possess to util-

THE ORDER OF VIRTUE

ize the environment, to turn it to its own advantage. This is the distinguishing and essential capacity of life in every form. A plant can continue to exist, and a sculptor can model a statue, only through being so organized as to be able to assimilate what the environment offers. Whether it be called tropism or technique, it is all one. Intelligence in this sense may be said to be the elementary virtue, conditioning success on every plane of activity.

In using such terms as "satisfaction" and "success" interchangeably with so irreproachable a term as "fulfilment," I may, until my meaning is wholly clear, seem to degrade morality. But the tone of disparagement in these first two terms is due to their having acquired certain arbitrary associations. It is supposed that to be satisfied is to be complacent, and that to be successful is to be hard and worldly. Now, a narrow satisfaction and a blind success are morally evil; but satisfaction and success may be taken up into a life that is wholly wise and devoted. They will, in fact, constitute the real body of value in any practical enterprise, from the least to the greatest.

The absence of intelligence, which I shall term *incapacity*, is the one absolutely fatal defect from which life may suffer. Incapacity embraces maladaptation, dulness, feebleness, sickness, and death. Like its opposite it does not enter into the moral account except in so far as it affects a group of interests, through being prejudicial to an individual's efficiency or a community's welfare; but it will impair and annul attainment upon any plane. The fault of incapacity attaches not only to life that is rudimentary or defective, but also to the mechanical processes which have not been assimilated to any interest and thus lie outside the realm of value. Incapacity in this sense is that metaphysical evil of which philosophers speak. It testifies to the fact that the cosmos is only partially subject to judgments either of good or of evil; that value has a genesis and a history within an environment that is at best plastic and progressively submissive.

In terms of intelligence and incapacity, the basal excellence and the basal fault, it is possible to define that whole affair of which morality is the constructive phase: the attempt of life to establish itself in the midst of primordial lifelessness, to avert dissolution and death, and to extend and amplify itself to the uttermost.

Within the economy of the simple interest there is no possibility of formalism, since there is no subordination of interest to anything higher than itself. But we meet here with materialism in its purest form. *Overindulgence* is the fault which attaches to the exclusive insistence of the isolated interest on itself; when it grows headstrong, and is like to defeat itself through being blindly preoccupied.

The evil of overindulgence arises from two natural causes. In the first place an interest is essentially self-perpetuating; in spite of periodic moments of satiety, an interest fulfilled is renewed and accelerated. Just in so far as it is clearly distinguished it possesses an impetus of its own, by which it tends to excess, until corrected by the protest of some other interest which it infringes. Overindulgence is most common where such consequences are delayed or obscured by artificial means; hence its prevalence among those who can afford for a time to dissipate their strength, or have some means of replenishing it. And imprudence is common where the penalty is insidious. The corruption entailed by gluttony, inebriety, and incontinence may be slow and doubtful, or apparently remitted in moments of recovery; but if one indulge himself in foolhardiness or violence, he is like to be repaid on the spot. Hence the latter forms of imprudence are more rare. To avoid imprudence, it is necessary to discount that aspect which the interest wears within the period of its immediate fulfilment, and thus avoid the necessity of repeating the hard and wasteful lesson of experience. This truth, which is the first principle of all practical wisdom, has been graphically represented in Jeremy Taylor's *Rules and Exercises of Holy Living:*

> Look upon pleasures not upon that side that is next the sun, or where they look beauteously, that is, as they come towards you to be enjoyed; for then they paint and smile, and dress themselves up in tinsel and glass gems and counterfeit imagery; but when thou hast rifled and discomposed them with enjoying their false beauties, and that they begin to go off, then behold them in their nakedness and weariness. See what a sigh and sorrow, what naked and unhandsome proportions and a filthy carcass they discover; and the next time they counterfeit, remember what you have already discovered, and be no more abused.[3]

There is a second source of overindulgence in the ever-increasing complexity of the moral economy. The more numerous the interests, the more difficult the task of attending to their connections and managing their adjustment. Not only is the need of prudence never outgrown; it steadily acquires both a greater urgency and a greater difficulty.

If incapacity may be said to be the metaphysical evil, the taint of the cosmos at large, overindulgence may be said to be the original sin, the taint of life itself. It is life's offence against itself, the denial of greater life for the sake of the little in hand. It is the perennial failure of the

THE ORDER OF VIRTUE 87

individual interest to unite itself with that universal enterprise of which it is the microcosmic image.

III

The simplest *moral* economy is that in which two or more interests are *reciprocally adjusted* without being subordinated. The principle of organization which defines such an economy is *prudence*. Prudence becomes necessary at the moment when interests come into such contact with one another as provokes retaliation. Thus, for example, interests react on one another through being embodied in the same physical organism. Each bodily activity depends on the well-being of co-ordinate functions, and if its exercise be so immoderate as to injure these, it undermines itself. *Moderation* gains for special interests the support of a general bodily health.

But bodily health is not the only medium of interdependence among the interests of a single individual. His interests must draw not only upon a common source of vitality, but also upon a common stock of material resources. The limitation of interests that follows from this fact is frugality or *thrift*, the practical working of the principle that present waste is future lack, and that, therefore, to save now is to spend hereafter. Thrift involves also a special emphasis on livelihood, since this is a source of supply for all particular interests.

The social relation makes interests externally interdependent in a great variety of ways. Interests must inhabit one space, exploit one physical environment, and employ a common mode of communication. If any interest so acts as unduly to divert one of these mediums to its own uses, it must suffer retaliation from the other interests that likewise depend on that medium. It is prudent to give even one's rival half the road, and to divide the spoils with him. There is a politic form of *honesty;* and *veracity* may be conceived only as a kind of caution. Thus Menander says: "It is always best to speak the truth in all circumstances. This is a precept which contributes most to safety of life." [4] *Tact* is only a more refined method of avoiding the antagonism of interests that operate within the same field of social intercourse.

The economy of prudence has its own characteristic value. Indeed, if this were not so there would be no possibility of that form of baseness known as being *merely* prudent. There is a prudential equilibrium; a condition of smooth and harmonious adjustment, within the personal life or the community. I propose that this equilibrium be termed *health*. In that admirable idealization of renaissance morality, Castigli-

THE ORDER OF VIRTUE

one's *Book of the Courtier*, the author refers to the immediate reward of self-control that comes both from inner harmony and the approbation of one's fellows. To instil goodness into the mind, "to teach continence, fortitude, justice, temperance," Castiglione would give his prince "a taste of how much sweetness is hidden by the little bitterness that at first sight appears to him who withstands vice; which is always hurtful and displeasing, and accompanied by infamy and blame, just as virtue is profitable, blithe, and full of praise." [5]

Socially, the healthful equilibrium corresponds to that "peace" which Hobbes praised above all things; [6] and which is all that is asked for by those who wish to be let alone in order that they may pursue their own affairs. Although such peace may be ignominious, it need not be so; and a sense of security and reciprocal adjustment must remain among the surviving values, whatever higher achievements be added to it. But the inherent value of health is most clearly defined by a nice equilibration of activities within the medium of the individual organism. I borrow the following description of health in this sense from a recent book by H. G. Wells:

The balance as between asceticism and sensuality comes in, it seems to me, if we remember that to drink well one must not have drunken for some time, that to see well one's eye must be clear, that to make love well one must be fit and gracious and sweet and disciplined from top to toe, that the finest sense of all —the joyous sense of bodily well-being—comes only with exercises and restraints and fine living.[7]

The temperance praised by the Greeks is of like quality, with a further reference to the reasonableness which it fosters. A prudence which is mastered, which has become a spontaneity, delivers reason from bondage, and makes the whole of life easily conformable to it. Thus Castiglione, who is so often reminiscent of Plato and Aristotle, draws a contrast between continence, as the "conquest" of prudence, and temperance as its "beneficent rule."

Thus this virtue does not compel the mind, but infusing it by very gentle means with a vehement belief that inclines it to righteousness, renders it calm and full of rest, in all things equal and well measured, and disposed on every side by a certain self-accord which adorns it with a tranquillity so serene that it is never ruffled, and becomes in all things very obedient to reason and ready to turn its every act thereto and to follow wherever reason may wish to lead it, without the least unwillingness.[8]

Such is that prudence which, though rich in its own right, is nevertheless subordinate to greater good.

It is proper to regard prudence as inferior in principle to purpose and good-will, or even as ignoble when confirmed in its narrowness. It

THE ORDER OF VIRTUE

denotes an organization of life in which as yet no interest has risen above the rest; it bespeaks the common populace of interests, disciplined, but not moved to any eminent achievement. The fact that the validity of the principle of prudence is so readily granted is significant of this. Prudence requires no interest to be other than itself, but meets it on its own ground. There is no elevation of motive.

But prudence is the first and most instructive lesson in morality. It has a peculiar impressiveness, not only because it is so promptly and unmistakably verified, but because it is so close to life. Its meaning is unlikely to be obscured through being abstracted from the real interests whose saving is the proof of its virtue. Furthermore, although prudence is not the highest principle in life, it is a mistake to suppose that it is therefore unnecessary in the highest spheres of life. There is a problem of prudence that underlies every practical problem whatsoever. If interests are to be organized they must be not only subordinated but also co-ordinated, that is, adjusted within every medium in which they meet. Without moderation, caution, self-control, thrift, and tact there is no serving man or God. As life increases in complexity it is easy to forget these basal precepts. Nature has provided a model, both simple and fundamental, in physical health.

"The body," says Burke, "is wiser in its own plain way, and attends its own business more directly than the mind with all its boasted subtilty."[9]

The prudential organization of life furnishes the first type of *formalism*. Prudence requires that the interest shall be limited in order that it may not antagonize other interests and thus indirectly defeat itself. Discipline is justified, in other words, by its fruits. But discipline involves an initial moment of negation, in which the movement of the interest is resisted. It must be checked, and its headway overcome, if it is to be redirected. The exaggeration of this moment of negation, or a steady persistence in it, is *asceticism*. Its fault lies in its emptiness, in its destruction or perversion of that which it was designed only to protect against itself.

Asceticism appears most frequently as a subordinate motive in some general condemnation of the world on religious grounds, and must receive further consideration in that connection. Its proper meaning as a purely prudential formalism is best exhibited in the Greek Cynics. These philosophers were moved to mortify the flesh, and to deny their social interests, by extreme caution. They discovered that the safest method of adjustment was simplification. If one permits one's self no desires, one need not suffer from their conflict, nor need one treat with the desires of others. Now this would be a very perfect solution of the problem of adjustment, if only there were something left to adjust. If a Cynic can attain to a state of renunciation in which he wants nothing, he will be sure of having what he wants; only, unfortunately, it will be nothing. Epictetus has thus represented the Cynic's boast:

> Look at me, who am without a city, without a house, without possessions, without a slave; I sleep on the ground; I have no wife, no children, no prætorium, but only the earth and heavens, and one poor cloak. And what do I want? am I not without sorrow? Am I not without fear? Am I not free?

Now it is clear that the sum of the Cynics' attainments is not large. It consists, indeed, almost wholly in a certain hardened complacency, and a freedom to make faces at the world. To the onlooker, whose comment Epictetus also records, their aspect is mean:

> No: but their characteristic is the little wallet, and staff, and great jaws; the devouring of all that you give them, or storing it up, or the abusing unseasonably all whom they meet, or displaying their shoulder as a fine thing.[10]

In other words, since the Cynic continues to live after having rejected the proper instruments and forms of life, he must make a living out of the charitable curiosity excited by his very unfitness.

And asceticism of this prudential type tends always to be both empty and monstrous; empty because it denies life, and monstrous because life is not really denied, but only perverted and awkwardly obstructed.

There is a materialistic evil corresponding to the prudential organization of life which is known as meanness, vulgarity, or *sordidness*. It denotes a failure to recognize anything better than the fulfilment of the simple interests in their severalty. Although guarded and adjusted these still determine the general tone of life. The controlling motive, the standard of attainment, is never anything higher than the elementary desire with its attendant satisfaction. In its negative aspect this is termed *aimlessness*, and is identical with the Christian vice of idleness, so graphically described by Jeremy Taylor:

> Idleness is called *the sin of Sodom and her daughters*, and indeed is *the burial of a living man*, an idle person being so useless to any purposes of God and man, that he is like one that is dead, unconcerned in the changes and necessities of the world; and he only lives to spend his time, and eat the fruits of the earth: like a vermin or a wolf, when their time comes they die and perish, and in the meantime do no good; they neither plough nor carry burdens; all they do is either unprofitable or mischievous.[11]

Thus aimlessness denotes a failure to attain anything of worth; a lack of consecutiveness and

THE ORDER OF VIRTUE

unity. The correction of this fault lies in a new principle of organization.

IV

This new principle of organization consists in the *incorporation o interests*, that is, their subordination to a *purpose* that embraces them, unifies them, and carries the whole to a successful issue. The incorporation of interests is peculiarly an intellectual process. It is this to which Socrates refers when he says that *knowledge is virtue*. Purpose requires, in the first place, that one should define and foresee the end, and in the second place, that one should be sagacious and watchful in the service of it. Purpose is the virtue of the understanding, of a mind which is adventurous enough to project an enterprise, but has enough of home-keeping wit to judge nicely of cause and effect or of part and whole.

There are many virtues which contribute to purpose, and of these none is more indispensable than *patience*, or the capacity to labor without hire for a prize deferred. "Better is the end of a thing," says the Preacher, "than the beginning thereof: and the patient in spirit is better than the proud in spirit." Steadiness of purpose under adverse or confusing circumstances is called *persistence*, *courage*, *loyalty*, or *zeal*, with differences of meaning that reflect the nature either of the purpose or the circumstances.

But since purpose is so much an intellectual virtue, special importance attaches in this economy to *truthfulness*. If one's purpose be some form of personal achievement, one must deal honestly with one's self. And this is not easily done. Epictetus told his pupils that men were loath to admit any fault that they held to be really blameworthy:

> Some things men readily confess, and other things they do not. No one then will confess that he is a fool or without understanding; but quite the contrary you will hear all men saying, I wish that I had fortune equal to my understanding. But men readily confess that they are timid, and they say: I am rather timid, I confess; but as to other respects you will not find me to be foolish. A man will not readily confess that he is intemperate; and that he is unjust, he will not confess at all. He will by no means confess that he is envious or a busybody. Most men will confess that they are compassionate.[12]

Now if one is to attain anything difficult, he cannot afford to indulge in vanity or self-satisfaction; for action can be kept true to its end only when the least obliquity is marked and corrected. Hence the strong man does not attribute his failure to fortune or to his amiable virtues, but to his folly; for he knows that to be the crucial fault which it lies within his power to remedy.

On the other hand, if the purpose be one

which involves the co-operation of several persons, it is necessary that these should deal openly and candidly with one another. Truthfulness is a condition of any collective undertaking. It is interesting to observe the growing recognition of the need of publicity wherever democratic institutions prevail. Secrecy is a sort of treason. If men are to work together for their common welfare they must be truly in touch with one another; otherwise there is a spy at their councils, an incalculable force that may counterwork their plans.

Achievement, the value which the virtue of purpose conditions, needs no moralist's justification. The world never tires of praising it, for it is the world's business. By achievement I mean the fulfilment by subordinated and cumulative effort of an interest deliberately adopted for its greatness of value. Life is now controlled not by the accident of desire, but by the due preference of the better. It has begun to be rational not only in its method, but also in its aim. It is now more fruitful, because more broadly conceived, being engaged in enterprises which continue, and which draw from many sources. Hence a man can better endure the spectacle of his own life, for it seems not to be wholly mean or ineffectual. In that his conduct is unified, consistent, and directed to some worthy end, he is possessed of that quality of *character* which is respected in him both by himself and by his fellows.

It is unfortunate that there is no better term than *sentimentalism* with which to indicate that variety of formalism which is characteristic of the purposive economy. The fallacy consists essentially in the abstraction of the purpose from its constituent interests. The true value of a purpose lies in its function of organization; and is, therefore, inseparable from the interests to which it gives unity and fulfilment. But its form, or even its mere name, may, through association, come to acquire a fictitious value. When this fictitious value gives rise in contemplation or discourse to a certain emotional satisfaction, we employ the term "sentimentalism" in the conventional sense. This is the sentimentalism of those

"Who sigh for wretchedness, yet shun the wretched,
Nursing in some delicious solitude
Their slothful loves and dainty sympathies."

I wish, however, to emphasize a more insidious variety of this error, in which it may be more profoundly and fatally confusing. I refer, in the first place, to what may be described as *deferred living*. There is a popular illusion to the effect that a life purpose is to be fruitful only at the end; that it is something to be prepared for in youth, worked for in maturity, and attained—

THE ORDER OF VIRTUE

well, it is difficult to say when. This is the fallacy of heaven transferred to earth. "Man never is, but always to be blest." Life is conceived as a sentence at hard labor, the only sure compensation being the ultimate deliverance. Now there is but one justification of a life purpose, and that is its conserving of the whole of life; it must save each day and each hour. There is no more virtue in the future than in the present. "The greatest disaster," says a Greek proverb, "is for a man to be opened and found empty"; and this does not refer to an autopsy. It is at least one function of a life-purpose to make life distributively and continuously good. That one's life shall be pointed with a purpose does not mean that it shall be reduced to a point. The very virtue of organization lies in its making room for the free play of immediate and particular interests, in its surrounding them at a distance with invisible safeguards.

A second important case of sentimentalism is *nationalism*. The value of the state lies in its protection and development of the concrete life of the community. The true object of patriotism is social welfare. But for the state as a provident economy, there may be substituted as an object of loyalty what is only an idea or a name; and when this is done men are easily persuaded to play into the hands of unscrupulous leaders.

To the abominable tyrannies which have thus been made possible I need not refer. In Hegel's philosophy of history,[13] as well as in many modern political theories, this error has been deliberately affirmed. But for illustration I prefer to turn to the case of Plato. The *Republic* was conceived, it is true, without bias of party or race, but there is none the less a strain of arbitrariness and illiberality in it. This is due to the fact that the state is conceived by itself, with a quality and perfection of its own that displaces the interests of its citizens.[14] A state which is defined otherwise than as a provision for the very diversity of life, an organization responsive to pressure from every constituent desire, fails from over-simplification. This I take to be the meaning of Aristotle's comment on the *Republic*:

> The error of Socrates must be attributed to the false notion of unity from which he starts. Unity there should be, both of the family and of the state, but in some respects only. For there is a point at which a state may attain such a degree of unity as to be no longer a state, or at which, without actually ceasing to exist, it will become an inferior state, like harmony passing into unison, or rhythm which has been reduced to single foot. The state is a plurality, which should be united and made into a community by education.[15]

There is a chapter in the *Discourses* of Epictetus, entitled: "To or against those who obstinately Persist in what they have determined."

THE ORDER OF VIRTUE

There could, I think, be no better formulation of purpose grown hard and unworthily self-sufficient. This form of materialism I have termed *egoism* and *bigotry*, since the purpose may be either personal or social in scope. But in either case the diagnosis of Epictetus goes to the root of the evil. He thus describes his experience with one of his companions, "who for no reason resolved to starve himself to death":

> I heard of it when it was the third day of his abstinence from food, and I went to inquire what had happened.
> "I have resolved," he said.
> "But still tell me what it was which induced you to resolve; for if you have resolved rightly, we shall sit with you and assist you to depart; but if you have made an unreasonable resolution, change your mind."
> "We ought to keep our determinations."
> "What are you doing, man? We ought to keep not to all our determinations, but to those which are right; for if you are now persuaded that it is right, do not change your mind, if you think fit, but persist and say, we ought to abide by our determinations. Will you not make the beginning and lay the foundation in an inquiry whether the determination is sound or not sound, and so then build on it firmness and security?" . . .
> Now this man was with difficulty persuaded to change his mind. But it is impossible to convince some persons at present; so that I seem now to know, what I did not know before, the meaning of the common saying, That you can neither persuade nor break a fool. May it never be my lot to have a wise fool for my friend: nothing is more untractable. "I

am determined," the man says. Madmen are also; but the more firmly they form a judgment on things which do not exist, the more ellebore they require.[16]

The wise fool is, as Epictetus says, more intractable than the aimless and unwitting fool; because there is substance to his folly. There is at least some truth on his side. But his folly is folly none the less. He hardens himself against that which would save him; while boasting himself a lover of light, he shuts his eyes lest any ray of it penetrate to him. Thus the egoist, through the atrophy of his sympathies and his preoccupation with a narrow ambition, gratuitously impoverishes his life; and it is difficult to convince him of his loss, because he indubitably has some gain.

Bigotry consists essentially in the failure to employ the method of discussion, in the failure to recognize in every rational being a possible source of that truth which all need. It is a stupid forfeiture or waste of the resources of intelligence possessed by one's fellows. The King Creon of Sophocles's *Antigone* is a masterly representation of the futility of this pride of opinion. Creon angrily resents every impeachment of his wisdom, insisting on instant and unquestioning obedience. But his son Haemon thus attempts to save him from himself:

Father, the gods plant wisdom in mankind, which is of all possessions highest. In what respects you

THE ORDER OF VIRTUE

have not spoken rightly I cannot say, and may I never learn; and still it may be possible for some one else to be right too. . . . Do not then carry in your heart one fixed belief that what you say and nothing else is right. For he who thinks that he alone is wise, or that he has a tongue and mind no other has, will when laid open be found empty.[17]

It was once a practice even among learned men to set personal pride above the truth. The chancellor of the University of Paris complains of this practice in the Middle Ages:

What are these combats of scholars, if not true cock-fights, which cover us with ridicule in the eyes of laymen? A cock draws himself up against another and bristles his feathers. . . . It is the same to-day with our professors. Cocks fight with blows from their beaks and claws; "Self-love," as some one has said, "is armed with a dangerous spur."[18]

Egoism and bigotry, then, consist essentially in the exaggeration and immobility of an adopted purpose. As is the case with every variety of materialism, their fault lies in their blindness, in their fatuous rejection of the good that is offered to them. But this is not all. For in denying the good which is offered to him, the egoist or bigot also virtually denies the reason which offers it. It is this that constitutes the affront which is called *injustice*.

The full meaning of injustice has been recognized only gradually, and it is even now by no means free from confusion. But I think that it will be agreed that the sting of it is a failing in respect. Violence may be wholly without this taint; and the most bitter injustice may be wholly without violence. To be unjust is to be condescending or supercilious; to assume superiority on personal grounds, ignoring the equal access to truth which is enjoyed by every rational being. The nice quality of injustice is most clearly to be apprehended where it is accompanied by benevolent intent. It is one of the princely attributes described in the *Book of the Courtier*, and justified in a manner that leaves no doubt of its implied meaning:

> True it is that there are two modes of ruling: the one imperious and violent, like that of masters toward their slaves, and in this way the soul commands the body; the other more mild and gentle, like that of good princes by means of laws over their subjects, and in this way the reason commands the appetite; and both of these modes are useful, for the body is by nature created apt for obedience to the soul, and so is appetite for obedience to reason. Moreover, there are many men whose actions have to do only with the use of the body; and such as these are as far from virtuous as the soul from the body, and although they are rational creatures, they have only such share of reason as to recognize it, but not to possess or profit by it. These, therefore, are naturally slaves, and it is better and more profitable for them to obey than to command.[19]

Now the essence of injustice lies in this Platonic manner of classifying human beings in terms of limited capacities; in assigning to some the degraded status of the appetites, and to others a limited faculty of understanding, while arrogating to a few the full power and title of Reason. The resentment of this arrogance is no more than the assertion of that potentiality of reason which distinguishes the animal man; it is his inevitable coming of age, his determination to play the man's part.

V

Justice is the mutual respect through which rational purposes enter into a relation of *fraternal equality*. It is the courteous paying of honor where honor is due. In modern times justice has very properly been identified with *tolerance*, which is the acknowledgment that one is one's self equally liable to error with another, and that another is equally liable to truth with one's self. Justice attaches a certain finality to the judgment of every individual instrument of reason. Under the form of justice *veracity* realizes its highest meaning. The truth is not to be administered with paternal indulgence or caution; it is to be yielded as a right to every free and self-determining mind.

The practice and the spirit of justice pervade every highly developed social grouping, such as marriage, friendship, or fellow-citizenship in a democracy. For Aristotle a friendship is "one soul dwelling in two bodies"; [20] that is, the same high capacity uniting two individuals in the acknowledgment of its common principles, and in the contemplation of its common objects. Aristotle's other saying, that "man is a political animal," is inspired with the same meaning. To participate in the life of a state, in which one's fellow-citizens were one's equals, in which men with equal endowments carried on one united activity while acknowledging one another's independence, was to an Athenian the very fulness of life. To be banished from it was, even in the eyes of the law, equivalent to death.

In a chapter of his *Physics and Politics*, entitled "The Age of Discussion," Bagehot has admirably represented the importance for human progress of an open exchange of opinion on all matters of great consequence:

In this manner all the great movements of thought in ancient and modern times have been nearly connected in time with government by discussion. Athens, Rome, the Italian republics of the Middle Ages, the *communes* and states-general of feudal Europe, have all had a special and peculiar quickening influence, which they owed to their freedom, and which states without that freedom have never communicated. And it has been at the time of great epochs of thought—at the Peloponnesian War, at the fall of the Roman Republic, at the Reformation, at the French Revolution—that such liberty of speaking and thinking have produced their full effect.[21]

THE ORDER OF VIRTUE 107

Elsewhere Bagehot attributes to freedom of discussion, not only the deliverance from narrow and conventional habits, but that general elevation of tone which is characteristic of such an era as the Elizabethan age in England. In short, justice or toleration, since it encourages men to push on to the limit of their powers, promotes not only originality and diversity, but a love of perfection.

It will have been observed that justice and freedom are complementary, for he who is just liberates, and he who is free receives justice. Together they constitute the basis of all the higher relationships between men, of a progressive society, and of the whole constructive movement which we call civilization.

But it is possible to construe justice and freedom only negatively, as meaning that the individual is to be allowed to go his way in peace. Such a misconception is formalistic, in that it rests on a failure to recognize the providence or fruitfulness of justice. The virtue of justice lies not in its disintegration of society, but in its enabling the members of society to unite upon the highest plane of endeavor. Justice is a method wherewith men may profit collectively, and in their organized effort, from a sum of enlightenment to which every individual contributes his best. *Anarchism* rests in the negative protest against conformity; forgetting that the only right to liberty is founded on the possession of a reasonableness that inclines the individual to the universal; and forgetting that the only virtue in liberty lies in the opportunity for union and devotion which it provides.

There is a more restricted form of anarchism in *scepticism* which attaches finality to differences of opinion, and overlooks the fact that these very differences must be regarded as converging approaches to the common truth. For men can differ only in the presence of identical objects which virtually annul their difference. To be free to think as one pleases cannot but mean to think as truly as possible, and so to approach as closely as possible to what others also tend to think.

But a larger importance attaches to that mild variety of anarchism which is commonly called *laissez-faire*, and which Matthew Arnold calls British Atheism or Quietism. The reader will recall Arnold's quotation from the *Times:*

> It is of no use for us to attempt to force upon our neighbors our several likings and dislikings. We must take things as they are. Everybody has his own little vision of religious or civil perfection. Under the evident impossibility of satisfying everybody, we agree to take our stand on equal laws and on a system as open and liberal as is possible. The result is that everybody has more liberty of action and of speaking here than anywhere else in the Old World.

THE ORDER OF VIRTUE

And from Mr. Roebuck:

> I look around me and ask what is the state of England? Is not every man able to say what he likes? I ask you whether the world over, or in past history, there is anything like it? Nothing. I pray that our unrivalled happiness may last.[22]

This is an almost perfect representation of the sentimental interest in justice. In the course of such justice, "none of us should see salvation." It leaves wholly out of account the fact that when men are left free to talk or act or live as they will, they will either stagnate, or they will strive for the best and help it to prevail. If the latter, they will be brought back to the *state as the means of making right reason effective*, and of extending to all not simply the leave to be what they want to be, of following what Arnold calls their "natural taste of the bathos," but the opportunity of learning better.

Justice, like purpose and prudence, is a principle of organization, owing its virtue to the larger fulfilment of interest which it makes possible. Through this principle the individual is granted independence, in order that his freedom may remove every limit from his service. He is delivered from the bondage of violence and convention, but he is delivered into the charge of his own reason, which must give bonds not only that he will keep the peace, but that he will give himself wholly to that true good which he may now discern.

In justice the human secular society is perfected. By a secular society I mean a society held to be self-sufficient as it is; a society in which only those interests are acknowledged which are actually present, or have actually been admitted to a place of power or prestige. But secularism or *worldliness* in this sense suffers from the general error of materialism, the error of mistaking the *de facto* good for the whole good. It is only another case of that blindness which is the penalty of all self-sufficiency. The ancient and the modern types of worldliness present an interesting difference which will serve to illustrate their common fault.

Greek literature abounds in the glorification of the life already achieved. Thus Solon asks no more of the gods than to be fortunate and honored: "Grant unto me wealth from the blessed gods, and to have alway fair fame in the eyes of all men. Grant that I may thus be dear to my friends, and bitter to my foes; revered in the sight of the one, awful in the sight of the other." [23]
To this Pindar adds the petition that, "being dead I may set upon my children a name that shall be of no ill report." [24] Even the ideal of the philosophers is only a refinement of this; recog-

THE ORDER OF VIRTUE

nizing the superiority of such activities as engage the imagination or reason, but nevertheless finding happiness to be complete in terms of the fulfilment of the dominant desires within the existing political community. This conception was vaguely distrusted, it is true; but it represents the characteristic enlightenment of the most enlightened centre of Greek life. Its insufficiency was not clearly demonstrated until the advent of Christianity; when it was proved to lie in a lack of *pity*. Now pity is not, as is sometimes supposed, a kind of weakness; it is a kind of knowledge, wherewith men are reminded of obscure and neglected interests. It is easy to understand why the Christian revolution should have been regarded as destructive of culture. For it meant not the qualitative refinement of the good, but the quantitative distribution of it. But it none the less marks an epoch in moral enlightenment; since the bringing of all men up to one level of opportunity and welfare is as essential a part of the good as the cultivation of distinction.

The modern worldliness consists not in a lack of pity, but in a lack of *imagination*. Philistinism, as Matthew Arnold describes it, is a complacent satisfaction with the *kind* of good that is praised and sought for in any given time. Such complacency is found in its most extreme form among those reformers or even religious leaders who are devoted to the saving of men; for these come to overrate their wares through the very act of pressing them upon others. Matthew Arnold never tires of illustrating this from the Liberal propaganda of his day:

> And I say that the English reliance on our religious organisations and on their ideas of human perfection just as they stand, is like our reliance on freedom, on muscular Christianity, on population, on coal, on wealth—mere belief in machinery, and unfruitful; and that it is wholesomely counteracted by culture, bent on seeing things as they are, and on drawing the human race onwards to a more complete, a harmonious perfection.[25]

In other words, both humanism and humanitarianism may be lacking in humanity: humanism, on account of its insensibility to pain and hunger and poverty when these lie outside a narrow radius of bright intensive living; humanitarianism, on account of its failure to honor the highest type of attainment and to prefigure a perfection not yet realized.

VI

There is but one economy of interests which furnishes the proper sphere of moral action, namely, the *universal* economy which embraces within one system all interests whatsoever, present, remote, and potential. The validity of this economy lies in the fact that the goodness of action cannot be judged without reference to all the interests affected, whether directly or indirectly. To live well is to live for all life. The control of action by this motive is the virtue of *good-will*. It should be added that the good will must be not only compassionate, but just; offering to help, without failing to respect. And it must be not only devoted, but also enlightened; serving, but not without self-criticism and insight.

Such a programme need not seem bewildering or quixotic. If my action does not offend those most nearly concerned, it will scarcely offend those removed by space, time, or indirection. Charity begun at home is spread abroad without my further endeavor. Furthermore, it is good-will rather than a narrow complacency that inspires my assuming of the special tasks and responsibilities defined by proximity, descent, and special aptitude. Life as a whole is built out of individual opportunities and vocations. It is required only that while I live effectively and happily, as circumstance or choice may determine, I should conform myself to those principles which harmonize life with life, and bring an abundance on the whole out of the fruitfulness of individual effort.

Good-will is the moral condition of religion, where this is corrected by enlightenment. The religion of good-will is best illustrated, from the

European tradition, in the transition from paganism to Christianity. I have said that the Greeks were not without distrust of that natural and worldly happiness which they most praised. This, for example, is the testimony of Euripides:

> Long ago
> I looked upon man's days, and found a grey
> Shadow. And this thing more I surely say,
> That those of all men who are counted wise,
> Strong wits, devisers of great policies,
> Do pay the bitterest toll. Since life began,
> Hath there in God's eye stood one happy man?
> Fair days roll on, and bear more gifts or less
> Of fortune, but to no man happiness.[26]

This note of pessimism grows more marked among the philosophers, and is at length taken up into the Christian renunciation of the world. The philosophers attempted to devise a way of happiness which the superior individual might follow through detaching himself from political society and cultivating his speculative powers.[27] But the Christian renunciation involved the abandonment of every claim to individual self-sufficiency, even the pride of reason. It expressed a sense of the general plight of humanity, and looked for relief only through a power with love and might enough to save all. Hence there is this fundamental difference between pagan and Christian pessimism: the pagan confesses his powerlessness to make himself impregnable

THE ORDER OF VIRTUE

to fortune, while the Christian convicts himself of sin, confessing his worthlessness when measured by the task of universal salvation. The one pities and absolves himself; the other condemns himself.

Now the other-worldliness of Christianity was without doubt a grave error, which it found itself compelled to correct; but it was none the less the vehicle through which European civilization became possessed of the most important secrets of religious happiness. In the first place, all are made sharers, through sympathy, in the failure of the present; and, thus distributed, the burden is lightened. "It is an act within the power of charity," says Sir Thomas Browne, "to translate a passion out of one breast into another, and to divide a sorrow almost out of itself; for an affliction, like a dimension, may be so divided as, if not indivisible, at least to become insensible." [28] In the second place, it is understood that there is no such thing as a happiness that is enjoyed at the expense of others and by the special favor of fortune. There is no promise of individual salvation save in the salvation of all. A private and protected happiness is bound sooner or later to be destroyed by an increase of sensibility, by an enlightened awareness of the evil beyond. And to experience evil, to realize it, and yet to be content, lies not within the power of any moral being; it is not merely difficult, it is self-contradictory. To any one who judges himself fairly, with a wide and vivid image of life as it is in all its ramifications and obscurities, the evil of the world is all one. It follows that, as there is no perfect happiness except in the annihilation of evil, so there can be no peace of mind, no self-respect, no sense of living truly and for the best, unless one's action can be conceived as wholly saving and up-building, as contributing in its place and in its way to the general forward movement. This, I think, is the deeper explanation of the buoyancy of devoted people, of that buoyancy which was a source of such great wonder to the disillusioned wise men of ancient times. And this, I think, is the meaning of the Christian teaching that it is more blessed to give than to receive; and that the love of one's God is to grow out of the love of one's neighbor.

I have endeavored to show that the highest good is the greatest good; that it may not only be inferred from the present good, but that it actually *consists* of the present good, with more like it, and with the present evil eliminated. By *mysticism* I mean that species of formalism in which the highest good, out of respect for its exaltation, is divorced from the present good, and so emptied of content. Professor James has said that it is

THE ORDER OF VIRTUE

characteristic of rationalists and sentimentalists, to "extract a quality from the muddy particulars of experience, and find it so pure when extracted that they contrast it with each and all its muddy instances as an opposite and higher nature." [29] There is a peculiar liability to such abstraction in religion, for religion involves a judgment of insufficiency against every limited achievement. A longing after unqualified good is the very breath of enlightened religion; and in order that that ideal may be kept pure, it must not be identified with any partial good. Indeed, the office of religion requires it to condemn as only partial, good that is commonly taken to be sufficient. Now there is only one way of defining a good that shall be universal without being merely formal, and that is by defining perfection quantitatively rather than qualitatively; substituting for the Platonic Absolute Good, in which the present good is refined away into a phrase or symbol, the maximum good, in which the present good is saved and multiplied. He who believes that he conceives goodness otherwise than as the good which he already possesses, deceives himself; as does the author of the *Religio Medici*, when he says:

That wherein God Himself is happy, the holy Angels are happy, in whose defect the Devils are unhappy, that dare I call happiness; whatsoever conduceth unto this may with an easy Metaphor deserve that name; whatsoever else the World terms Happiness, is to me a story out of Pliny, a tale of Boccace or Malizspini, an apparition, or neat delusion, wherein there is no more of Happiness than the name. Bless me in this life with but peace of my Conscience, command of my affections, the love of Thyself and my dearest friends, and I shall be happy enough to pity Cæsar.[30]

Now it is safe to say that Sir Thomas Browne was in fact unable to attribute to God and the angels any other happiness than these same blessings which he covets for himself, saving only that they shall be without stint, and joined with others like them.

Formalism, as we have seen, is never merely negative in its consequences; for any moral untruth, since it replaces a truth, cannot fail to pervert life. Thus one may be persuaded with the author whom I have just quoted to count the world, "not an Inn, but an Hospital; and a place not to live, but to dye in." [31] I do not suppose that any one ever succeeded in wholly resisting the hospitality of this world, and one suspects that Thomas Browne partook not a little of its good cheer; but the opinion is false notwithstanding, and if false, then confusing and misleading. This world is not a place to suffer in, nor even a place to be mended in, but the only opportunity of achievement and service that can be certainly

THE ORDER OF VIRTUE

counted on. The good is in the making here, if it is in the making anywhere. To neglect life here is equivalent to forfeiting it altogether.

Religious formalism may induce not only a default of present opportunity and responsibility, but also a substitution for good living of an emotional improvisation on the theme of absolute perfection, like that in the *Book of the Courtier*:

> If, then, the beauties which with these dim eyes of ours we daily see in corruptible bodies, . . . seem to us so fair and gracious that they often kindle most ardent fire in us, . . . what happy wonder, what blessed awe, shall we think is that which fills the souls that attain to the vision of divine beauty! What sweet flame, what delightful burning, must that be thought which springs from the fountain of supreme and true beauty!—which is the source of every other beauty, which never waxes nor wanes: ever fair, and of its own self most simple in every part alike; like only to itself, and partaking of none other; but fair in such wise that all other fair things are fair because they derive their beauty from it. This is that beauty identical with highest good. [32]

Now I do not want to be understood as condemning this mysticism out of hand. I mean only that while it is eloquent and purifying, it is, nevertheless, not illuminating; and that if it be mistaken for illumination, it does in fact hide the light. It has no meaning whatsoever except the general idea of the superlative, and if it be not attached to some definite content drawn from experience of acts and their consequences, it does but substitute a phrase for the proper objects of action and an emotion for provident conduct.

There is a further moral danger in mysticism, which I need only mention here, because I propose to discuss it more fully in the chapter on religion. Since mysticism opposes a formal perfection to the concrete good of experience, it tends to obscure the distinction between good and evil. That distinction lies within experience, and if experience as a whole be discredited, the distinction is discredited with it. If the common, familiar good is not to be taken as valid, then finality no longer attaches to that common, familiar evil which the moral will has been trained to condemn and resist. If the good lie "beyond good and evil," then neither is the good good nor the evil evil. The result is to leave the moral will without justification, supported only by habit and custom.

The virtue of piety lies in its completing, not in its replacing, secular efficiency. It gives to a life that is provident and fruitful as it goes, the stimulus of a momentous project, and reverence for a good that shall embrace unlimited possibilities.

THE ORDER OF VIRTUE

VII

In reviewing the several levels of life which morality defines, we may observe two types of universal value. The lower values in relation to the higher are indispensable. There is no health without satisfaction, no achievement without health, no rational intercourse without achievement, and no true religion except as the perfecting and completing of a rational society. The higher values, on the other hand, are more universal than the lower in that they surpass these in validity, and are entitled to preference. Thus the lower values are ennobled by the higher, while the higher are given body and meaning by the lower. Satisfaction derives dignity from being controlled by the motive of good-will, while the moral kingdom at large derives its wealth, its pertinence to life, and its incentive, from the great manifold of particular interests which it conserves and fosters.

It is the formal rather than the material principle in life which defines the direction of moral effort. By prudence, purpose, justice, and good-will life is regenerated and urged, against the resistance of inertia, towards its maximum of attainment. Hence these are the virtues which make men heroes, and which are symbolized in manners and in worship. Manners are a symbolic representation of rational intercourse; thus courtesy is a ceremony of respect, chivalry of service, and modesty of self-restraint and impersonality. Worship is similarly a symbolic representation of good-will and hope. Upon the cultivation of "those outward and sensible motions which may express or promote an invisible devotion" human life is dependent not only for its graciousness, but for its discipline and growth.

CHAPTER IV

THE MORAL TEST OF PROGRESS

I

THE phrase "philosophy of history" is at present somewhat in disrepute. It enjoys much the same unpopularity among historians as does the term "metaphysics" among scientists, and probably for the same reason. It is assumed that such a discipline must either violate or exceed the facts in the interests of some *a priori* conception. Doubtless some philosophies of history have been guilty of this charge; but they do not, I am sure, exhaust the possibilities in the case. In the present chapter I shall present an outline of what might fairly be regarded as a philosophy of history, but which nevertheless does no more than attempt a precise definition of principles which even the historian is forced to employ.

I shall not attempt to define the task of history, except in the broadest terms. The form which its results should finally assume is a matter of dispute among historians themselves. But it is at least possible to indicate the field of history in terms that will command general assent. In the first place, history deals with change, with the temporal sequence of events; and in the second place, it confines itself to such events as belong to what is called human conduct. Entirely apart from theories of method or technique, it seems clear that any established fact falling within this description belongs properly to that body of knowledge which we call history.

I wish especially to call attention to the fact that history deals with *human conduct*. It deals, in other words, with actions which serve interests; with needs, desires, and purposes as these are fulfilled or thwarted in the course of time. Its subject-matter, therefore, is moral. It describes the clash of interests, the failure or success of ambition, the improvement or decay of nations; in short, all things good and evil in so far as they have been achieved and recorded. And the broader the scope of the historian's study the more clearly do these moral principles emerge. The present-day emphasis on the accurate verification of data somewhat obscures, but does not negate the fact, that every item of detail is in the end brought under some judgment of good or evil, of gain or loss in human welfare. All history is virtually a history of civilization; and civilization is a moral conception referring to the sum of human achievement in so far as this is pronounced good.

Now there is a branch of philosophy called

MORAL TEST OF PROGRESS

"ethics," to which is committed the investigation of moral conceptions. These conceptions are as much subject to exact analysis as conceptions of motion or organic behavior. And such an analysis must underlie all judgments concerning the condition of mankind in any time or place, if these judgments make any claim to truth. The application of ethical analysis to the recorded life of man is a philosophy of history.[1] Such a discipline is charged with the criticism of the past in terms of critical principles which have been explicitly formulated. With a knowledge of what it means to be good or evil one may conclude in all seriousness whether the fortunes of society in any time or place were good or evil. One may with meaning distinguish between those who have been the friends and the enemies of society; and one may refer to the growth or decay of nations with some notion of what these terms signify. But it will be the main problem of a philosophy of history to deliver some verdict concerning the progress or decline of institutions, and of civilization at large.

It is necessary that we should at once rid our minds of false notions concerning the meaning of *progress*. This conception has been greatly confused during recent times through being identified with evolution in the biological sense. It should be perfectly clear that such evolution may or may not be progressive; it means only a continuous modification of life in accordance with the demands of the environment. Even where this modification takes the direction of increasing complexity it does not necessarily constitute betterment; and it is entirely consistent with the principle of adaptation that it should take the reverse direction. Biological evolution signifies only a steady yielding to the pressure of the physical environment, whether for better or for worse. It is also important not to confuse the conception of progress with that of mere change or temporal duration. Because society has grown older it has not necessarily on that account grown wiser; nor because it has changed much has it necessarily on that account changed for the better. Whether the accumulations of the past are wealth or rubbish is not to be determined by their bulk.

Progress cleared of these ambiguities means, then, *a change from good to better;* an increase, in the course of time, of the *value* of life, whatever that may be. Taken in the absolute sense it means, not a gain here or a gain there, but *a gain on the whole*. It is impossible to reach any conclusion whatsoever concerning progress except in the light of some conception of the total enterprise of life. Every advance must be estimated not merely in relation to the interest immediately served, but in relation to that whole complex of interests which is called humanity.

In discussing progress I shall therefore with right employ those moral conceptions which I have already defined. I shall regard as good whatever fulfils interests, and as morally good whatever fulfils all interests affected to the maximum degree. Especial importance now attaches to the principle which I have phrased *the quantitative basis of preference*. Since progress involves the change from good to better, it implies an increment of value. The later age is judged to be *as good and better*. I can see no way of verifying such a proposition unless it be possible to find in the greater good both the lesser good and also something added to it and likewise accounted good. In other words, progress involves measurement of value, and this involves some *unit of value* which is common to the terms compared. The method must be in the last analysis that of superimposition.

Bagehot virtually employs this method in the chapter of his *Physics and Politics*, which he entitles "Verifiable Progress Politically Considered." Let me quote, for example, his comparison of the Englishman with the primitive Australian.

If we omit the higher but disputed topics of morals and religion, we shall find, I think, that the plainer and agreed-on superiorities of the Englishmen are these: first, that they have a greater command over the powers of nature upon the whole. Though they may fall short of individual Australians in certain feats of petty skill, though they may not throw the boomerang as well, or light a fire with earthsticks as well, yet on the whole twenty Englishmen with their implements and skill can change the material world immeasurably more than twenty Australians and their machines. Secondly, that this power is not external only; it is also internal. The English not only possess better machines for moving nature, but are themselves better machines. Mr. Babbage taught us years ago that one great use of machinery was not to augment the force of man, but to register and regulate the power of man; and this in a thousand ways civilized man can do, and is ready to do, better and more precisely than the barbarian. Thirdly, civilized man has not only greater powers over nature, but knows better how to use them, and by better I here mean better for the health and comfort of his present body and mind. He can lay up for old age, which a savage having no durable means of sustenance cannot; he is ready to lay up because he can distinctly foresee the future, which the vague-minded savage cannot.[2]

It will be observed that in each case the superiority of the Englishmen lies in the fact that they *beat the Australians at their own game*. Australians are as much interested as Englishmen in obtaining command over nature, in organizing their own powers, and in securing health and comfort. The Englishmen, however, can fulfil these interests not only up to but also beyond the point which marks the limit of the Australians' attainment.

The method of superimposition is virtually employed in all competitive struggle. The glory and fruits of victory are sought by both opponents, and the success of one is the failure of the other. The superiority of the victor to the vanquished is beyond question only because they had the same interest at stake.

The application of this method to the determination of progress is not confined to philosophers of history. It is applied by every individual who realizes that his advance from childhood to maturity has been attended with growth and development. For the old boundaries of childhood still remain as evidence of the greater magnitude of the life which has outgrown them. Similarly every man may mark within himself the various limits which once bounded him, but which he has since exceeded in consequence of steady and consecutive effort. The progress of mankind at large differs only in complexity and range. It can be tested and determined only because identical interests persist. If men had not in all times wanted the same things it would be impossible to measure their attainments. Their successes and failures would be incommensurable. But the old needs and the old hopes yet remain. The problem of life which was from the beginning is a problem still. If it can be shown that the old needs are met more easily, along with new needs besides, that there is better promise that the hopes will be fulfilled, and that the general problem of life is nearer a solution, then human progress will have been demonstrated.

II

I propose, in the first place, to discuss two general principles, the operation of which is conducive to progress. One of these principles is *external*, that is, it relates to the environment of life rather than to its internal economy; and to this I shall turn first.

The external environment of life is in some respects favorable, in other respects unfavorable. Now, strangely enough, it is the unfavorable rather than the favorable aspect of the environment that conduces to progress. Progress, or even the least good, would, of course, be impossible, unless the mechanical environment was morally plastic. The fact that nature submits to the organization which we call life is a fundamental and constant condition of all civilization. But there is nothing in the mere compliance of nature to press life forward. It is the *menace* of nature which stimulates progress. It is because nature always remains a source of difficulty and danger

MORAL TEST OF PROGRESS

that life is provoked to renew the war and achieve a more thorough conquest. Nature will not permit life to keep what it has unless it gains more.

The external environment of life embraces not only mechanical nature, but also such outlying units of life as have not yet been brought into harmonious relations. Conflict between individuals, tribes, races, or nations operates in a manner analogous to mechanical nature. It exerts a constant pressure in the direction of greater strength and efficiency. In order that man shall not be robbed by his enemies of what he already has, he must forever be attempting to make himself impregnable and formidable.

But war and the struggle with nature not only put a premium on the better organization of life; they also make it a condition of permanence. Superior individuals survive when inferior individuals perish in the struggle, or the superior type obtains an ascendency over the inferior. In human warfare the defeated party is rarely if ever utterly annihilated; it tends, however, to lose its prestige or even its identity through being assimilated to the victorious party. In either case that form of life which in conflict proves itself the stronger, tends to prevail, through the exclusion of those forms which prove themselves weaker.

An unfavorable environment has, then, operated externally to develop coherence and unity in life. But the cost has been prodigious, and must be subtracted from the gain. For there is no virtue in conflict save the strength of the victor. Man has made a virtue of this necessity; but to obviate so dire a necessity becomes one of the first tasks which civilization undertakes. The attempt to eliminate conflict, and reduce to a minimum the sacrifice of special interests, marks the operation of the *internal* or *moral* principle of progress. During the historical period this principle assumes a constantly greater prominence.

A society may be said to be internally progressive when it can afford to withdraw some of its energies from the struggle for existence, and devote them to the improvement of method and the saving of waste. Its stability and security must be so far guaranteed as to make it safe to undertake a reconstruction, calculated to provide more fully for its constituent interests and develop its latent possibilities. There now obtains, within limits that tend steadily to expand, what Bagehot calls "government by discussion," that is, the regulation of action by the invention, selection, and trial of the best means. This substitution of rational procedure for custom is an irreversible and germinal process. Let me quote Bagehot's account of it:

A government by discussion, if it can be borne, at once breaks down the yoke of fixed custom. The

MORAL TEST OF PROGRESS 133

idea of the two is inconsistent. As far as it goes, the mere putting up of a subject to discussion is a clear admission that that subject is in no degree settled by established rule, and that men are free to choose in it. . . . And if a single subject or group of subjects be once admitted to discussion, ere long the habit of discussion comes to be established, the sacred charm of use and wont to be dissolved. "Democracy," it has been said in modern times, "is like the grave; it takes, but it does not give." The same is true of "discussion." Once effectually submit a subject to that ordeal, and you can never withdraw it again; you can never again clothe it with mystery, or fence it by consecration; it remains forever open to free choice, and exposed to profane deliberation.[3]

The strength of custom or established authority lies in prompt and undivided action against external enemies; but its weakness lies in its excessive cost to the interests within. And when there is leisure and security for deliberation, the policy and organization of society must respond at once to the claims of these interests. Development is now due to a moral rather than to a mechanical principle; that is, the surviving type of life is due not to pressure and elimination from without, but to a provident concern that emanates from within. There is a deliberate intention to promote survival, those interests alone being restricted or suppressed which do not comply with this intention. There evolves not a selected group of strong individuals, but a strong community, strong because both full of life, or rich in incentive, and also harmonious. And within such a community the strength of individuals lies not in a sheer power to resist the strain of competition, but in the rational and moral capacity to utilize the resources of the entire community. Through moral organization the strong are made stronger at the same time that the weak are made strong.

Strictly speaking, there is only one internal principle of progress, namely, *rationality*. By rationality, in this connection, I mean the knowledge of the good, and the correction of existing usages through which it is accidentally or wantonly frustrated. If fulfilment be the motive of life, and maximum fulfilment be the good, then any existing usage stands condemned when it is proved to involve unnecessary sacrifice. And such usages will be condemned, and in the long run rejected, wherever there is an opportunity for self-assertion and discussion among the various interests concerned. But such correction may be initiated either by a positive or a negative motive. It may result either from the action of those who seek constructively to promote the general welfare of society, or from the action of those who protest against society in behalf of neglected interests. The first is *constructive reform*, the second, *revolution*.

Constructive reform is the work of disinterested

reflection. It may originate in speculation, as political or social theory; or it may originate in the solution of a practical problem. Plato has described the type of mind which in either case it requires: a mind which is free from individual or party bias, and which represents and co-ordinates all the interests of the community. Now the failure of political and social theories as measures of reform is proverbial; none failed more completely and conspicuously than Plato's own. And it is not difficult to see why this should be the case; for, as a rule, they are adapted neither to the habits and intelligence of the time, nor to the actual instruments of practical efficiency. But it may be observed that the distance between the philosopher and the man of affairs is considerably shorter than it used to be. The method of discussion being once generally adopted, action, both individual and social, is pervaded with theory. Even the man of affairs cannot easily avoid being a philosopher.

And even in distinguishing as sharply as I have between theory and practice, I have simply followed a customary habit of thought that is on the whole misleading. For, in truth, it is as impossible for the man of affairs to avoid disinterested reflection, as it is for the commercial traveller to be unsociable. The activity of the one has to do with the organization of a wide range of interests, as the activity of the other has to do with the capitalization of good-fellowship.

Those of you who are familiar with the First Book of Plato's *Republic* will remember the account given there of the forced benevolence of the tyrant. It is, I believe, one of the great classics in ethical theory; and although its full meaning will not appear until we deal directly with the problem of government, I must allude to it here for the sake of the principle involved. The sophist of the dialogue, one Thrasymachus, attempts to overthrow Socrates's conclusion that virtue is essentially beneficent, by pointing to the case of the tyrant, who is eminent and powerful, as every one would wish to be, but who is at the same time wholly unscrupulous. He is the symbol of success, in that he can on all occasions do what it pleases him to do, and with no regard for the feelings of others. Now Socrates in his reply is not satisfied to show that even the tyrant must have some scruples; he goes to the length of asserting that the tyrant must of all persons in the community have the *most* scruples. And the reason which Socrates advances is unanswerable. The tyrant is the one person in the community who has to *please everybody*. He owes his position and power, not to any directly productive activity, such as agriculture, industry, or military service, but wholly to his skill in organizing and promoting interests that are not primarily his own. To be sure, he has his hire; but to earn it he must pay every man his price.

Now let us apply this to the general case of the man of affairs. It follows that just in so far as action is broad in scope, it must be considerate and just. To conduct enterprises on a large scale involves contact with many interests, and these interests, once affected, must either be understood and provided for or else antagonized. The greater the enterprise, the more truly does it exist by sufferance; it depends on the support of those who profit by it, and if that support be withdrawn, it collapses into absolute impotence. The ancient Cynics were right in thinking that the only man who can afford to be indifferent to the interests of his fellows is the man who renounces ambition and retires to his tub.

Once the era of civilization is inaugurated, power depends on moral capacity, that is, the capacity to protect and promote a considerable number of interests, and thus win their backing. This is proved in every field of human activity, military, political, religious, intellectual, social, or commercial. Commerce and industry afford at present the most striking examples. The man who succeeds is the man who can satisfy the greatest number of appetites. And the more his enterprise grows the more it becomes a public concern;

and the more, therefore, must he be studious of public welfare and responsive to public opinion. Thus manufacturing, transportation, or banking, when conducted on a large scale, touch life at so many points, that he who seeks to gain power or wealth by means of them will gradually and without any abrupt change of motive approximate the method of disinterested service. So every station in life, from that of the ruler to that of the shopkeeper, has its own characteristic form of the one problem of *meeting, adjusting and fulfilling interests*. The desire to be successful or to attain eminence in one's station exerts a constant pressure in the direction of the invention, trial, and selection of methods that will solve this problem. And such methods once devised are at once supported by the interests they serve, and become necessary to the life of the community.

Now the wise leader anticipates the needs and wishes of his followers, and so enjoys their continued support without ever seeming to depend on it. But there are very few such wise leaders. The reason for their scarcity lies in the natural inertia of profitable activities. There is a universal propensity to let well enough alone. So methods are allowed to outlive their usefulness, or remain unmodified when more provident and fruitful methods could be devised. When leader-

MORAL TEST OF PROGRESS 139

ship thus fails to be statesmanlike and far-sighted, there occurs that uprising of the disaffected interests which is called *revolution*.

Revolution, then, is the self-assertion of the various constituent interests which do not find room or fair measure within the existing organization. The evidence of the insufficiency of present methods being neglected by those in charge, that evidence *makes itself* known. In the long run this is the surest principle of progress, because it is brought into operation by those who have a nearer or more indispensable interest at stake. It is unquestionably to the interest of the individual who heads an enterprise to conduct it rationally, that is, to make it always as productive as possible for all the interests which it serves. But if he fails he may not at once incur the penalty, or be conscious of it if he does; he may only forfeit an increase of power, or render his position precarious. On the other hand, to the constituent interest which is sacrificed, this same failure may mean loss of bread or even loss of life. Hence the latter is more sure to move in the matter. Justice is more urgently needed by the slave who rebels, than by the master who may be brought through enlightenment to liberate him. Thus neglected interests have been the conscience of every great human reform. Let me cite the two greatest cases of this in the history of European civilization, Christianity and the French Revolution.

Christianity as a social revolution was a protest against the existing order on the part of interests which it did not recognize. I do not mean that these interests were not tolerated; they were, of course, protected, and even given a legal status. But in the reckoning of good and evil they were not *counted*. Women and slaves, the poor, the ill-born, and the ignorant, were instruments which the happy man might use, or incidents of life which might test his charity and magnanimity. These classes rose to overthrow no single institution, but a whole conception of life, or standard of well-being which was defined to exclude them. In paganism, which did not pass with the advent of Christianity, but still lingers as the creed of the very precious souls, humanity is conceived only qualitatively, and not quantitatively. The good of the race is conceived to consist in the perfection of a few, chosen for their superior endowment and fortune. The eminent refinement and nobility of these demigods is substituted for the saving of lives, for the general distribution of welfare and opportunity. The many are to find compensation for their hardship in the happiness of the few. But the Christian principle of atonement was the precise opposite of this: one suffered that all might be blessed. Christianity looked towards a good that should number every one in the multitude and endure throughout all time. Now it has since appeared that this was no more than the truth; and that it might have been conceived and executed by the wise men, had they only been more wise. But they were wise only within the limits of their own conceit. Hence it took the form of an assault on the established enlightenment. The many, with their yearning for a universal happiness, with their deep concern for the greater good, and their jealous compassion for all souls, destroyed the narrow eminence of the few. Thus Christianity was a revolution, and not a constructive reform.

The French Revolution was a protest not only against apathy, but against insolence as well. It was a demand of the many not merely to be happy, but to have what they called their "rights" respected; a protest against authority, not only because it was cruel, but because it was arbitrary, tyrannical. Hence it was aimed against priestcraft as well as against monarchy. It was based on the conviction that no one is so justly entitled to pass judgment on a man's affairs as a man himself. But it was a cry from the depths, the bitter resentment of a long-standing abuse. Therefore it took the form of an uprising against the established order; and while it opened men's eyes, it was not conducted in the spirit of enlightenment. In spite of his inferences, Nietsche has not described the matter falsely:

> The slave . . . loves as he hates, without *nuance*, to the very depths, to the point of pain, . . . his many *hidden* sufferings make him revolt against the noble taste which seems to *deny* suffering. The scepticism with regard to suffering, fundamentally only an attitude of an aristocratic morality, was not the least of the causes, also, of the last great slave insurrection which began with the French Revolution.[4]

Insurrection, in other words, is the flat, downright, and unqualified affirmation of interests to which those in charge of affairs have denied existence. It is a flash in the eyes of those who will not see; a blast in the ears of those who will not hear. Insurrection asserts *only* the interests that have been neglected; hence, though it brings *new* light, that light for lack of which the world went in darkness, it is careless and blind in its own way, and does not concern itself with restoring the balance. But, as Nietsche prefers not to comprehend, insurrection demonstrates beyond question the bankruptcy of aristocratic morality; discredits it as effectually, and in the same way, as new evidence discredits old theories.

These, then, are the two complementary methods through which rationality gets itself progressively established: through the imagination and foresight of constructive minds, and through the protest or uprising of neglected interests.

MORAL TEST OF PROGRESS 143

I must mention briefly, before leaving this general topic, an accessory condition on which this internal principle of progress depends for its effectual working. It is necessary that the life of society should be unbroken; that its achievements should be preserved and accumulated from generation to generation. This is provided for in the permanence of records, monuments, and institutions; but these are of less consequence than the *continuity of tradition.* Generations of men do not come into being and pass away like regiments in marching order. There is no present generation; unless one arbitrarily selects those of a certain age to represent the spirit of the day. He who is born now, enters into the midst of a social life in which the present is blended with the past through the interpenetration of individual lives of every stage of maturity. The threads are innumerably many, and their length is but threescore years and ten; but there is no place at which more than a few end, so that they are woven into one continuous and seamless fabric. It does not exceed the facts, then, to say that the life of society is one life, which may gather headway, increase in wealth, and profit by experience. Through this continuity society may learn, as the individual organism does, by the method of trial and error. Costly blunders need not be repeated, and the waste involved in untried experiments may steadily be reduced. Furthermore, the advance is by geometrical, and not merely by arithmetical progression. Every discovery and achievement is multiplied in fruitfulness through being added to the capital stock and reinvested in fresh enterprises.

III

Human progress, thus determined by the movement of life towards its more rational, that is, more provident, organization, is attended in all its stages with a very significant difference of emphasis. I refer to the old conflict between *conservatism* and *radicalism*. If this were merely a difference of temperamental bias, it would not need to detain us. But it is really an opposition between exaggerated truths, in which each is boldly and impressively defined.

The truth of conservatism lies, first, in its love of the existing order. Every established form of social life has had a certain wholeness and strength and perfection of its own. This is as true of savagery as it is of any type of civilization. Interests are in equilibrium, and are guaranteed security within certain limits that are generally understood. In other words, *at least a measure of fulfilment may be counted on.* The conservative is right in valuing this as a prodigious achievement. He knows that disorder is ruin, not to any class, but to all; the paralysis, if not the absolute destruction, of all fruitful activities.

And secondly, conservatism proclaims the truth that since order conditions all activity, it is impossible to promote human welfare except by *using* order. The enemy of order threatens to destroy the instruments of power, and so to make himself weak and helpless with the rest. The conservative understands the real delicacy of these instruments, and the difficulty of remodelling them while still forced to use them. For nothing puts so great a strain on society as progress. It tends to destroy its rigidity, to dull its edge, and to spoil the fine adjustment without which so complex an organization cannot function. There could be no human life whatsoever, and still less a progressive life, were not the great mass of men content to remain steadily in their places, and so form parts of a stable structure. An organization cannot actually *work* until it is in equilibrium.

Now while the conservative fears to "swap horses while crossing the stream," the radical reminds him that if he does not do so he will never gain the farther shore. The conservative is satisfied to sit firmly in the saddle, but the radical thinks only of the long distance yet to go. There is a common misconception as to who is the real radical, the real menace to this existing order.

He is not the sceptic, but *the man with a purpose;* the man who believes in the possibility of better things, and so has a motive impelling him to abolish and reconstruct the present things. The sceptic, who holds all order to be conventional and arbitrary, is as well satisfied with one system as another. His natural course is a cynical acquiescence in the inveterate folly of mankind. Or, finding order convenient, and fearing that its true groundlessness will be exposed if it be made a matter for discussion, he advocates blind obedience to the authority of the day. Hence the disillusioned, especially if they occupy positions of power in church or state or trade, may be counted on as the leaders of conservative policy. The typical radical, on the other hand, is Socrates, who censured the men of his time because they were satisfied with something short of the best; and who was condemned because he offered men *a good reason* for reorganizing life.

The radical, like the conservative, is right. He is right, in the first place, because he points out that the stability of the established order is not proof of its finality. It may be, indeed always will be, largely due to habit. Society forfeits a greater good through mere inertia, through the tendency of any organization of interests which runs smoothly and brings a steady return, to perpetuate itself. The radical is the critic of custom, condemning it for timidly clinging to the present good, and abandoning the original intent of life to attain to the maximum.

The radical is right, secondly, because he protests that so long as there is the least waste of life, the least wanton suppression or destruction of interests, the work of civilization is not done. He represents those interests which under any system are most heavily taxed, and presses for their relief.

Conservatism and radicalism, then, are the two half-truths into which the principle of progress is divided by the propensity of every human activity to override the mark, and by the confusion of mind that cannot fail to attend so venturesome and bewildering an undertaking as civilization.

IV

I have said that it is possible to measure progress because of the persistence throughout the whole course of human history of certain identical interests and purposes. When such an interest or purpose is sufficiently broad in its scope, and gets itself permanently embodied, it is called an *institution*. Thus *government* embodies the need of the general regulation of interests within the social community. *Education* is due to the individual's prolonged period of helplessness and dependence, and the need of assimilating him to the order of his time. *Science* is man's knowledge of the ways of nature in detail, when this is recorded, organized, and preserved as a permanent utility answering to the permanent need of adaptation. And *religion* expresses in outer form the human need of reckoning with the final day of judgment, of establishing right relations with the powers that underly and overrule the proximate sphere of life. There is no limited number of institutions, but these are notable examples. Government, education, science, and religion are fixed moral necessities. They arise out of those conditions of life which are general and constant. Hence each has a history coextensive with the history of society itself. And since the function of each remains identical throughout, the adequacy with which at any given time it fulfils that function may be taken as a measure of civilization. Government being the most prominent of institutions, and its improvement being the deepest concern of society, I shall select it for special consideration.[5]

I have already referred to the Platonic account of government, given in the *Republic*. It furnishes the starting-point of all political philosophy. In the First and Second Books, Plato examines two contrary sceptical criticisms of government, with a most illuminating result. In the First Book the sceptic urges the view that government represents the interest of the strong;

primarily of the ruler himself, enabling him to aggrandize himself at the expense of the weak. But in the Second Book the sceptic is made to suggest that government represents rather the interest of the weak, since it affords him a protection which he is not strong enough to afford himself. Now the moral of this paradox lies in the fact that government represents the interest neither of the strong nor of the weak, but of the community as a whole. This moral is virtually pointed in the reply which Plato makes to the first of these two sceptical positions. The ruler gains his power and prestige not from the exploitation of the interests of his subjects, but from his protection of them. His activity touches all the interests of the community, and is tolerated only in so far as it conciliates them. In other words, his strength is drawn wholly from the constituency which he serves. The many individual interests, on the other hand, owe their security to that concentration and organization which centres in the ruler. They only participate in a power which the ruler may exercise and enjoy as a unit. But unless that power be engaged in their service it ceases to exist. It is not a personal power, but a permanent function, through which the many interests of society unite, and so share severally the security, glory, and resourcefulness of the whole body.

Government in this sense is both a necessity and an opportunity. Suppose men to be in contact through propinquity or common descent. Divided among themselves they are prey to natural forces, wild beasts, or human enemies. But acting as a unit they are sufficiently strong to protect themselves. He who wields them as a unit to this end is for the time-being the ruler; and to submit to his leadership is simply to submit to the necessity of protection. Or, divided among themselves, they remain in a condition of poverty and fear; while united they can wage an aggressive campaign against nature, and against those who threaten them or possess what they lack. Again, he who settles their internal differences, accomplishes their organization, and makes it effective, is their ruler; and he owes his authority to the opportunity of conquest which his leadership affords.

The fact that government is thus of natural origin, the inevitable solution of an inevitable problem, has been obscured through confusing its general necessity with the accidental circumstances connected with the selection of rulers. The first ruler may have been appointed by God; or, as is more likely, he may have owed his choice to his own brutal self-assertion. But this has no more to do with the origin of the function of government, than the present methods of ambitious

MORAL TEST OF PROGRESS

politicians have to do with the constitutional office of a republican presidency. Government meets a moral need; and no man has ever ruled over men who has not met that need, however cruel and greedy he may have been in his private motives.

From the very beginning, then, government exists by virtue of the good that it does. But there have been enormous differences in the price that men have paid for that good; and this constitutes its variable and progressive factor. Tyranny is, in the long run, the most unstable form of government, because it grossly overestimates the amount that men will pay for the benefit of order. In the *Antigone* of Sophocles, Creon thus justifies his rule:

Than lawlessness there is no greater ill. It ruins states, overturns homes, and joining with the spear-thrust breaks the ranks in rout. But in the steady lines what saves most lives is discipline. Therefore we must defend the public order.

But when his son Hæmon protests against his tyranny, Creon states his understanding of the bargain:

CREON
Govern this land for others than myself?
HÆMON
No city is the property of one alone.
CREON
Is not the city reckoned his who rules?
HÆMON
Excellent ruling—you alone, the land deserted![1]

In other words, Creon does not understand that if he exacts everything he will possess nothing. There will come a point when the cost to the community exceeds the gain; and when that point is reached government must either make more liberal terms or forfeit its power.

The principle of rationality in government is parsimony. When its benefit involves a wasteful sacrifice of interests and may be purchased more thriftily, the pressure of interest inevitably in the long run brings about the change. The interests upon which the burden weighs most heavily constitute the unstable factor, and since, in order that equilibrium may be restored, these must be relieved, there is necessarily a gradual liberalization of governmental institutions. In the light of these general considerations I wish briefly to examine three historical types of government, and then to present a summary of present tendencies.

There is an interesting estimate of the benefits and cost of the *ancient military monarchy* in the history of Israel, as recorded by the writer of the Book of Samuel. The elders have demanded that Samuel make them a king, to judge them, "like all the nations." But he first warns them of the price that they will have to pay:

And he said, This will be the manner of the king that shall reign over you: he will take your sons, and

MORAL TEST OF PROGRESS

appoint them unto him, for his chariots, and to be his horsemen; and they shall run before his chariots: and he will appoint them unto him for captains of thousands, and captains of fifties; and he will set some to plow his ground, and to reap his harvest, and to make his instruments of war, and the instruments of his chariots. . . . And he will take your fields, and your vineyards, and your oliveyards, even the best of them, and give them to his servants. . . . And he will take your men servants, and your maidservants, and your goodliest young men, and your asses, and put them to his work. He will take the tenth of your flocks: and ye shall be his servants. And ye shall cry out in that day because of your king that ye shall have chosen you.

But the men of Israel were willing to pay even this price, saying:

Nay; but we will have a king over us; that we also may be like all the nations; and that our king may judge us, and go out before us, and fight our battles.[7]

The benefits of monarchy, in which Israel sought to emulate her neighbors, were *judgment* and *military prowess*. Even where the evils of tyranny were most aggravated these benefits actually accrued and constituted a rational ground of authority. The king was, at least in a measure, worthy of his hire. But the cost was extravagant; the king exacted a disproportionate share of the plunder, and reduced his subjects to a condition of personal bondage. In the great monarchies, such as Assyria, Egypt, Persia, and the Roman

Empire in its later period, the benefits of his rule were greatly attenuated before they reached to the depths and extremities of his kingdom, judgment being reduced to the caprice of an irresponsible officer, and military prowess to a faint reflection of national glory. Now the weakness of such a polity lay in its doubtful value to the governed, these failing to participate fairly in its achievements, and so lacking incentive to support it. There was no clear and convincing identification of individual interest and national purpose.

The strength of Greek and Roman oligarchies, on the other hand, lay in precisely this *morale*, or solidarity of interest. Their small size and racial homogeneity brought the ruler into direct relations with a constituency which was clearly conscious of its purpose and held him closely to it. So even where the kingship lingered on as a form, this polity was virtually a compact self-governing community. The benefits of government, to which every other interest was harshly subordinated, were still judgment and military prowess. But these benefits were effectually guaranteed; and the sacrifices which they required became a code of honor, both to be praised and gloried in as parts of happiness. Those who think that the Spartans felt their discipline to be essentially a hardship should read the song of Tyrtæus, which they recited in their tents on the eve of battle:

> With spirit let us fight for this land, and for our children die, being no longer chary of our lives. Fight, then, young men, standing fast one by another, nor be beginners of cowardly flight or fear. But rouse a great and valiant spirit in your breasts, and love not life when ye contend with men. And the elders, whose limbs are no longer active, the old desert not or forsake. For surely this were shameful, that fallen amid the foremost champions, in front of the youths, an older man should lie low, having his head now white and his beard hoary, breathing out a valiant spirit in the dust. . . . Yet all this befits the young while he enjoys the brilliant bloom of youth. To mortal men and women he is lovely to look upon, whilst he lives; and noble when he has fallen in the foremost ranks.[8]

But the cost is none the less heavy because it is not felt. In the first place, there was the cost untold to those whom the oligarchy held in subjection, a hundred thousand Messenians and twice as many Helots. Their unequal participation in the benefits of government, necessary though it may have been, lent instability to the whole polity. It was the menace of their resentment that forced upon their rulers a policy of perpetual vigilance and military discipline. And in the second place, there was the cost to the Spartan himself of attaining to a physical efficiency equal to that of ten Helots.

In the rival polity of Athens, the first of these abuses is only in a measure corrected. The liberal extension of the privileges of citizenship is the achievement of a later age. But the democracy of Athens did demonstrate the internal wastefulness of a polity dominated by purely military aims. The classic representation of this protest against sacrificing individual taste and capacity, together with all growth and abundance in the arts of peace, to the harsh rigors and passive obedience of a soldier's life, is to be found in Thucydides. In the funeral oration attributed to Pericles there is this account of the superiority of Athenian institutions:

> It is true that we are called a democracy, for the administration is in the hands of the many and not of the few. But while the law secures equal justice to all alike in their private disputes, the claim of excellence is also recognized; and when a citizen is in any way distinguished, he is preferred to the public service. . . . And we have not forgotten to provide for our weary spirits many relaxations from toil; we have regular games and sacrifices throughout the year; at home the style of our living is refined; and the delight which we daily feel in all these things helps to banish melancholy. . . . And in the matter of education, whereas they [the Spartans] from early youth are always undergoing laborious exercises which are to make them brave, we live at ease, and yet are equally ready to face the perils which they face. . . . If then we prefer to meet danger with a light heart but without laborious training, and with a courage which is gained by habit and not enforced by law, are we not greatly the gainers? Since we do not anticipate the

pain, although, when the hour comes, we can be as brave as those who never allow themselves to rest; and thus too our city is equally admirable in peace and in war. For we are lovers of the beautiful, yet simple in our tastes, and we cultivate the mind without loss of manliness. [9]

The political disorders of later Athenian history illustrate the difficulty of reconciling individualism with order and stability. But at the same time they prove that the task is a necessary one, and that until it has been successfully performed, government can enjoy at best only a false security. For no interests can safely be neglected, least of all those which arise from the natural activities of men and lie in the direction of the normal growth of human capacities.

Now these ancient polities illustrate the inevitable pressure in the direction of liberal government. The original and always the fundamental values of government are *order* and *power*. But these must be obtained with the minimum of personal exploitation on the part of the ruler; the function of government must be clearly understood and vigilantly guarded by a body of citizens who identify their interests with it. And secondly, order and power must be made compatible with individual initiative, with playfulness and leisure, and with the free development of all worthy interests. This pressure has been steadily operative in the evolution of modern political institutions.

But there has also been another force at work of equally far-reaching importance. This force is the modern idea of democracy, in which *justice is modified by good-will*. With the ancients justice meant "that every man should practise one thing only, that being the thing to which his nature was most perfectly adapted."[10] Equality upon the highest plane of human capacity was limited even in theory to a privileged class. But since the advent of Christianity it has never been possible for European society to acquiesce with good conscience in a limited distribution of the benefits of civilization. For the new enlightenment teaches that when men's potentialities are considered, rather than their present condition, *there are no classes*. As a consequence men demand representation not for what they are, but for what they may become if given their just opportunity. The body of citizens whose good is the final end of government virtually includes, then, all men without exception. It is no longer possible simply to dismiss large groups of human beings from consideration on grounds of what is held to be their unfitness. For they now demand that they be made fit. Burke expresses this enlightenment when he says, in speaking of the lower strata of society:

As the blindness of mankind has caused their slavery, in return their state of slavery is made a pretence of keeping them in a state of blindness; for the politician will tell you gravely, that their life of servitude disqualifies the greater part of the race of man for a search of truth, and supplies them with no other than mean and insufficient ideas. This is but too true; and this is one of the reasons for which I blame such institutions.[11]

And so does every man now demand of the community as a whole that he shall be permitted to share equally in its benefits, and also, in order that his claims may be represented, that he shall have a voice in its councils. Do not misunderstand me. I do not mean that all men, therefore, must here and now be held to be equal; but only that they must be held to be capable of being as good as the best until they have demonstrated the contrary by forfeiting their opportunity. Nor do I mean that all men must therefore be given the ballot. We are discussing a question not of instrument, but of principle. I do mean that there is an idea that the best of life is for all; and that if there are many that are incapable of entering into it, then they must be helped to be capable. And I mean, furthermore, that *this idea works irresistibly*. It commands the support of the whole army of interests. It will never be abandoned because it makes for the increase of life on the whole; and hence no social order will from henceforth be stable that is not based upon it.

This idea that all men alike shall be the beneficiaries of government, when taken together with the ancient ideas that government shall be directly responsible to its beneficiaries, and shall make as liberal an allowance as possible for their individual claims and opinions, constitutes the general principle upon which the progressive modern state is founded. Let me briefly recapitulate certain characteristics of the modern state [12] which indicate its recognition of this principle, and hence its advance on the whole over earlier types.

1. In the first place, the modern state is essentially a territorial rather than a racial or proprietary unit. In other words, it is clearly defined as a necessity and utility arising out of the circumstance of propinquity. If men are to cast in their lot together they must submit to organization, and obey laws promulgated in the interest of the community as a whole. To-day men understand that if they had no government it would be necessary to invent one; that the existing government, whatever divinity doth hedge it, is thus virtually the instrument of their needs.

2. Secondly, this moral function of government is emphasized through being largely freed from personal or dynastic connections and expressed as a constitutional office.

3. Thirdly, the requirements of justice and good-will are reconciled with order through the principle of representation. Without this prin-

ciple it would be impossible for societies large enough to afford men protection, to admit all men to a share in their positive benefits and to a voice in their councils. Representative government is a method of political procedure through which authority is made answerable in the long run to all interests within its jurisdiction. The more recent tendencies in democratic communities to modify the representative system indicate the direction in which the pressure of interests is still urging society forward. It is no longer a question merely of the extension of the suffrage, but of directness and publicity. The procedure of government being recognized as of vital importance to all citizens, it must be straightforward and businesslike, with its books constantly open to inspection. The present distrust in elected representatives is not a sign of reaction, but of the evolution of the democratic intelligence. Where the machinery of representation becomes wasteful and clumsy, it ceases to serve the community. But this may mean either direct legislation, that is, a direct participation in public affairs by the people at large, or the intrusting of these affairs to a few conspicuously responsible agents selected for their businesslike competence and owing their tenure of office to the consent of their constituency. These methods are entirely consistent with one another; and they owe their adoption entirely to their better execution of the intent of democracy. Both presuppose that political authority is empowered by all the interests of the community to serve them, and that these interests shall in the end decide whether or not that service is adequately performed.

4. Fourthly, the modern state lays a constantly greater stress on questions of internal policy, thus emphasizing its basal function of conserving and fostering the interests directly committed to its charge. It is less occupied with war, and more occupied with education, sanitation, the conservation of national resources, and the regulation of commerce and industry.

5. Fifthly, the sequel to this is the growing recognition of the folly and wastefulness of war. War is becoming a last resort, a hard necessity, rather than an opportunity of national glory. The growth of the idea of international peace, and the improvement and extension of the method of arbitration, are evidence of a yielding to the weight of the collective interests of humanity. They prove the priority of the principle of construction over that of destruction, and the essentially thrifty and provident function of the state.

The present form of progressive political institutions will serve as an index of the times and a pledge of the future. It reflects better than any other element of civilization that growth of liberality and solidifying of interests which is the deep current of progress. Human society is becoming one enterprise, provident of all existing interests and covetous of the best. Now I know that this is to many but a dreary spectacle. There are those who feel diminished by it, overwhelmed by numbers, and degraded to the low level of average capacity and average attainment. Therefore I wish in conclusion to deal further with this spirit of the age, to guard it against misunderstanding, and make its fine quality more apparent.

V

It is charged that modern democracy is contrary to enlightenment through subordinating the strong man to the multitude of weak men, or the wise man to the multitude of ignorant men. But the modern idea of justice is based fundamentally neither on the mere sentiment of pity nor on fear of the mob, but on love of truth, and respect for all organs that mediate it. Society cannot afford forcibly to repress the judgment of any individual or class, lest her deeds be deeds of darkness. The task of good living is a task of well-nigh overwhelming difficulty, because it requires that no interest shall be ignored, and yet that all interests shall be in unison. Interests left out of the account will inevitably assert themselves, and through their steady pressure or violent impact destroy the organization which has excluded them. Hence the need of an order that shall provide for its own gradual correction; stable enough for security, and pliant enough to yield without shock to the claims of neglected or abused interests.

This need underlies the modern sentiment of tolerance, and the love of all the liberties that give a hearing to any sincere demand: freedom of speech and press, the wide distribution of the franchise, and of opportunity for power. Contrary to a theory that philosophers have done much to support, democracy is not a method of confounding intelligence with the clamor of many voices, but a method of correcting the single intelligence by the report of whatever other intelligence may be most advantageously related to the matter at issue. Human intelligence must operate from a centre, and must always overcome an initial bias due to familiarity and proximity. The consensus of opinion, or public opinion, is not essentially a composite opinion, but a corrected opinion in which such accidents of locality cancel one another. The following justification of democracy, formulated by Matthew Arnold, lays bare its insistent and wholly incontrovertible motive:

If experience has established any one thing in this world, it has established this: that it is well for any great class or description of men in society to be able to say for itself what it wants, and not to have other classes, the so-called educated and intelligent classes, acting for it as its proctors, and supposed to understand its wants and to provide for them. They do not really understand its wants, they do not really provide for them. A class of men may often itself not either fully understand its own wants or adequately express them; but it has a nearer interest and a more sure diligence in the matter than any of its proctors, and therefore a better chance of success.[13]

This conception of democracy has come latterly to be as fine a point of honor as any article in the code of chivalry or noblesse. The arrogance that claims a superiority of class, and the obsequiousness that loves a lord, all this Nietschean "pathos of distance," whether felt from the heights or the depths, is sharply repugnant to a new gentility, that embraces all that have had the joy of promiscuous social intercourse. From this aristocracy no one is excluded that does not exclude himself through servility or superciliousness. Its distinction is liberality, that is, the habit of disputing questions and judging persons on their merits, with due allowance for that never wholly negligible possibility that the other man is right. Among those who are united by this spirit, there is one joke that is an unfailing touchstone and bond of union—the institution of *lèse-majesté*. It is a matter for unquenchable laughter, that superiority should require to be protected against inferiority by the enforced signs of respect, or by a hedge of reserve.

It is the ridiculousness of the haughty or the prostrate manner that is absolutely fatal to it. And its ridiculousness appears at the moment when you let in the light. Class elevation is pretence, not superiority; complacence, not wisdom; impudence, not power. But the contempt of the just man for the unjust is edged with knowledge. It arises out of a sense for things as they are: a recognition of the breadth and intricacy of life, compared with the pitifully small understanding of those who propose to regulate it on their own authority; of the vivid reality and worth of interests that do not exist for those whose claims are absolute, but who are only the hapless victims of a narrow and warping tradition.

Many think that the modern democracy is too easy-going; too much infected with charity. Now it is quite true that it means that no interest whatsoever shall be cut off through being forgotten or lightly estimated. The conscience of to-day expresses the persuasion that there is no stable happiness in any activity which entails cruelty, which has any other motive than to save. But this is no more than the full meaning of the Platonic dictum that "the injuring of another can be in no case just." [14] This sensitiveness to

MORAL TEST OF PROGRESS

life that is remote or obscure, this feeling for the whole wide manifold of interests, is not a weakness; it is enlightenment, a lively awareness of what is really relevant to the task of civilization. To imagine and think life collectively, with all its interests abreast, is only to measure up roundly and proportionately to the practical situation as it actually is. Upon a mind thus alive to the whole spectacle there at once flashes the awkwardness here, the waste there, as of an enterprise only begun. Let me allow another to interpret this latter-day conscience. I quote from *First and Last Things*, written by Wells:

> I see humanity scattered over the world, dispersed, conflicting, unawakened. . . . I see human life as avoidable waste and curable confusion. I see peasants living in wretched huts knee-deep in manure, mere parasites on their own pigs and cows; I see shy hunters wandering in primeval forests; I see the grimy millions who slave for industrial perfection; I see some who are extravagant and yet contemptible creatures of luxury . . . I see gamblers, fools, brutes, toilers, martyrs. Their disorder of effort, the spectacle of futility, fills me with a passionate desire to end waste, to create order, to develop understanding. . . . All these people reflect and are part of the waste and discontent of my life, and this coordinating of the species in a common general end, and the effort of my personal salvation are the social and the individual aspect of essentially the same desire.[15]

But it must not be thought that this is a matter of mere creature comfort, of distributing staple benefits for which men already have the appetite. For every step in the organization of life is attended with the growth of new interests, and especially of interests fostered or directly evoked by principles that have proved their moral virtue. Thus the forms of prudence and justice are supported by the immediate love of these things. And a growing rationality involves an increasing subtlety and delicacy in desires, the enrichment of life through the multiplication of such sources of satisfaction as are consistent with order and liberality. The true democracy is considerate not only of present interests, but also of the potentiality and promise of life.

Only when the imagination pictures life in these terms is it possible to avoid a sense of ignominy and irresponsibility. And, contrary to a common misconception, there is no other attitude that can reconcile one to the unavoidable participation in the common life of all men. Only when thus united with one's fellows in a spirited and ennobling enterprise can one endure their fellowship. Comrades in arms are not fastidious. If one confines one's self, on the other hand, to a cultivation of one's rarity, or to a company of choice spirits, not only do these values themselves grow stale and vanish away, but the remainder of mankind becomes a crowd, and civilization a tumult. The collective life of mankind ceases to be jarring and repugnant only at the moment when one enters into it and becomes infused with its morale.

There will be some in whom this prospect arouses no eagerness. The wise men of any day are, of course, agreed among themselves that the times are bad—that they are likely to be still worse after they, the remnant, have departed. But this is an opinion which most men acquire when they attain to maturity, and happily the world has long since seen that they cannot help it, and learned on that account not to take it to heart. The part of Cassandra is always being played somewhere by a gentleman of middle age with a ripe experience of life. But in any serious judgment concerning progress this bias of maturity must be overcome by the use of the imagination, by a rational estimate of human affairs in their broad sweep, or, if necessary, by an infusion of youthfulness. We shall wait long if we wait

> "Till old experience do attain
> To something like prophetic strain."

There is a more serious cause of hopelessness, in the complexity of modern civilization. Its very teeming life, its wealth, its multiplicity of activities and passions, overwhelm the mind in its moments of fatigue like a devouring chaos. One longs for the day when the house of civilization shall be completed, so that one may dwell in it in peace.

We are, it is true, in a time when there is still rough work to be done. But it is not blind work. Never has society been so clear as to its several special ends, never has so little effort been due to chance or compulsion. Nor is it ineffective work; for man now works with good tools and the help of many hands. And there is consolation in the fact that the foundations of civilization are laid wide and deep in charity and welfare. There remains the perpetual task of re-establishing a spiritual order which has been strained and wracked by the heaving of many forces. But when the sanctuaries and altars are restored it will prove to be a new order, richer, more liberal, and more complete than any since men began to live.

CHAPTER V

THE MORAL CRITICISM OF FINE ART

I

THERE are certain human activities which not only are of special interest on their own account, but also hold a position of pre-eminence in civilization. Such are science, philosophy, the love of nature, politics, friendly intercourse, and fine art. The last of these activities enjoys a peculiar distinction because it is monumental. It not only calls into play all of the more refined capacities, but also records itself in permanent and worthy form. Hence the fine art of any period comes to be taken as an index of its remove from savagery.

In submitting fine art to moral criticism, I shall use it as the best representative of the whole class of activities which I have just described. If we have not been wholly astray in our analysis of the good, it should appear that these activities owe their pre-eminence not to their bare quality or tone, but to their humanity, that is, to their connection with a harmonious, just, and progressive state of society.

It is hard for a moralist to approach such a subject without timidity, especially if he is concerned with his reputation for enlightenment. For there are many who think that it is a mark of intellectual emancipation to abandon moral standards altogether when dealing with the fine arts. Life itself, they remind us, is only the greatest of the fine arts; and if life can be called beautiful, the last word has been said. The man of taste and delicate sensibility is thus empowered to overrule the moralist, and replace with his ideal of grace and symmetry the harsh and clumsy scruples of conscience. Now it is doubtless true that when life is good, it is also beautiful; a life in which every activity is true, in which the medium of opportunity is formed to accord with the most noble purpose, may well exhibit a superlative grace and symmetry. But to be beautiful, life must be good *in its own way;* and the principles which define that way are the principles of morality. Furthermore, in order that life shall be beautiful it must be made an object of perception or contemplation; while, in order to be good, it must be *lived*. And the principles which define the living of life are moral.

The confusion of goodness with beauty is, therefore, doubly stultifying. On the one hand, it substitutes for the moral conception of value conceptions that morally are indeterminate. For grace and symmetry may be exhibited by life on any plane whatsoever, provided only that it acquires stability. Indeed, one who aims above all things to make his life beautiful, ought consistently to abandon the moral effort to bring life to its maximum of fulfilment, and cultivate perfection of form within the sphere of least resistance. It is proverbial that many lower forms of life are more beautiful than man, but it is not always seen that these are the stationary forms of life, wholly lacking in that principle of rational reconstruction which is the condition of moral goodness. On the other hand, the confusion of goodness with beauty tends to substitute appreciation for action, and thus to make of life a spectacle rather than an enterprise. Thus to replace ethical with æsthetic conceptions is to take the heart out of morality. Beauty is precisely as relevant to moral goodness as it is to truth; and if investigators were taught to devise the prettiest theory imaginable, the result would be no more fatal to knowledge than is æsthetic sentimentalism to life. To think conformably with reality is knowledge, and to act conformably with all interests is life. If beauty is to be added unto truth and goodness, it must come as the natural sequel to a single-minded fidelity to these motives.

But even if it be true that moral standards are absolutely independent of the standards proper to art, it is not yet clear that the moralist is justified in regarding his standards as more fundamental than those of art. He may be politely but positively informed that he is not to trespass. Now I feel that, after what has preceded, I am fortified against the charge of impertinence. Art is subject to moral criticism, because morality is nothing more nor less than the law which determines the whole order of interests, within which art and every other good thing is possible. It will scarcely be denied that art is an expression of interest, that both its creation and its enjoyment are activities, moods, or phases of life; and it follows that before this specific interest can be safely or adequately satisfied, it is necessary to fulfil the general conditions that underlie the satisfaction of all interests. It is as absurd to speak of art for art's sake as it is to speak of drinking for drinking's sake, if you mean that this interest is entitled to entirely free play. Art, like all other interests, can flourish only in a sound and whole society, and the law of soundness and wholeness in life is morality.

The claim of art to exemption from moral criticism is commonly due to one or both of these two forms of misapprehension.

In the first place, it is assumed that morality, too, is a special interest; and that if the artist or connoisseur lets the moralist alone, it is no more than fair that the moralist should let him alone. But this assumption is false; as false as though the athlete were to chafe at the warnings of his medical adviser on the ground that general health was irrelevant to endurance or strength or agility. Now, doubtless, an athlete may for a time neglect his general health with no noticeable diminution of his skill; but that is only because he already possesses the health to abuse. It still remains true that the principles of health which the trainer represents are the principles upon which his skill is fundamentally based. Nature has made him healthy according to these principles, and he simply does not recognize his debt to them. Similarly, art may flourish in spite of the neglect of social and individual well-being, so that the pleadings of the moral advocate seem irrelevant; but this is possible only because the social order is already established, and the personality formed, according to the very principles which the moralist is announcing. Art may dissipate moral health, but it nevertheless lives only by virtue of such a source of supply. The basal condition of art is not the element of social evil or morbid temperament that may attract attention, but the measure of soundness that nevertheless remains.

The second misapprehension that lends plausibility to the excuses of art is the assumption that the moralist is proposing to *substitute* his canons for those of art. Now it is entirely true that moral insight in no way equips one for connoisseurship. There is a special aptitude and training that enables one to discriminate in such matters. But the moralist is judging art *on moral grounds*. Hence he does not say, "I see that your painting is ugly"; but he does say, "I see that your painting, which you esteem beautiful (and I take your word for it), is *bad*." In the same way the moralist does not say to the self-indulgent man, "I see that you are not having a good time" (the self-indulgent man is likely to know better); but he says, "I see that it is bad for you to be having this particular kind of good time." In other words, for the moralist larger issues are at stake, and he is considering these on the grounds proper to them. He is charged with defining and applying the principles which determine the good of interests on the whole; and while his conclusions can never replace those of the expert within a special field, they will always possess authority to overrule them.

II

Since we are to be occupied mainly with the bearing of art on morality, I wish so far as possible to avoid debatable questions concerning the origin and ultimate meaning of art. But we can-

CRITICISM OF FINE ART

not proceed without agreeing on a use of terms. I shall attempt, therefore, to give a straightforward and empirical account of that which comes to be called art in the history of civilization.[1]

We have already had occasion to observe that from the very beginning life adapts the environment to its uses; that is, gives to matter and to mechanical processes a new form in which these fulfil interest. Thus an area of land deforested and cultivated, or two stones so hewn and fitted as to afford a grinding surface, take on the imprint of the human need for food. Now such reorganizations of nature as the farm or the mill, however crude they may be, are works of art in the broadest sense. And in this same sense all the tools, furniture, and panoply of civilization, from the most primitive to the most highly evolved, whatever without exception owes its form to its fulfilment of an interest, may with entire propriety be called art.

In the great majority of cases the work of art after being made is *used;* that is, it becomes an instrument in the making of something else. Such art is called useful or *industrial art.* But it sometimes happens that the work of art is valued, not as an instrument in the ordinary practical sense, but simply as an object to be experienced. In the Scriptural account of creation it is said that "God saw everything that he had made, and, behold, it was good." When the products of activity are thus found good in the beholding of them they become works of *fine art*.

It would be improper sharply to divorce these two motives, or to make one any more original than the other. The interest in the exercise of the sensibilities, or other powers of apprehension, is doubtless as primitive as any of the special interests of the organism; and it is improbable that man ever made anything without getting some satisfaction from looking at it or handling it or feeling it. Commonly the same object is both useful and beautiful; as was the case with the primitive religious dance, which at the same time indulged a taste for rhythm and served as a means of propitiating the gods.

But the motive of fine art becomes clearer when it is purer. Objects are then made with explicit reference to the interest taken in apprehending them. I do not mean that they cannot on that account be useful, for without doubt utility itself contributes to beauty; but only that they owe their form primarily to the æsthetic interest. The motive of fine art in its purity appears when special materials are selected on account of their plasticity and their appeal to the more highly developed senses. Fine arts that employ one medium are now separated and perfected through the cultivation of expert proficiency.

Thus there arise such arts as painting and music, one of which gives form to light and appeals to the eye, while the other gives form to sound and appeals to the ear. In this way society comes to acquire and accumulate objects which are designed, either wholly or in part, with reference to the special æsthetic interest. They are the creatures of this interest, and their place in life is determined by it. To understand their importance and to estimate their moral value it is therefore necessary to isolate this interest and examine it with some care.[2]

By the æsthetic interest I mean to refer to the interest that is taken in the work of fine art by the observer. There is undoubtedly a special interest in creation, but it is of relatively small importance. Even the artist is controlled largely by the interest in observing his own work; and art is a serious social concern only because of its appeal to the unlimited number of persons who may enjoy it without having any hand in the making. Now, in the passing allusion which I have made to the æsthetic interest, I have already used the term which is most convenient for purposes of general definition. The æsthetic interest is *the interest in apprehension*. What I mean by this will become clear when I compare it with two other interests which may also be taken in the content of experience. There is, in the first place, what is called the practical interest, that is, the interest in an object on account of what can be done with it by manipulation or combination with other objects. Secondly, there is the theoretical interest in the structure of reality, manifesting itself in the exploration of the object and its context. Now the interest in apprehension is not an interest in what can be done with the object, nor in its real structure, but in *the present conscious reaction to it*. One may take all three of these interests in the same object. Thus if I pluck the flower and take it home to my wife, I give evidence of a practical interest in it; if I kneel down and examine it carefully, I suggest the botanist; while if I continue to gaze at it where it lies, it would appear that I enjoy simply looking at it. It is this interest simply in looking at things, in just the perceiving, feeling, thinking, or imagining them, that I mean to sum up as the interest in apprehension, or the æsthetic interest. When objects excite this interest, when, that is, any state or process of consciousness of which they are the content tends to be prolonged for its own sake, they are said to be beautiful. And objects which are deliberately and artificially invested with a peculiar capacity to excite this interest are works of fine art.

I shall not undertake to explain the interest in apprehension further than to describe certain typical forms which it assumes. These forms will serve not only to illustrate its general meaning, but also to amplify that meaning in a manner that will prove important when we come to the discussion of moral questions. The forms which I shall mention are by no means exhaustive of the possible forms of the interest in apprehension, while the order that I shall follow is only roughly the order of increasing complexity.

There is, in the first place, an interest in *sensation*. I do not, of course, mean to assert that any state of purely sensuous enjoyment is possible; but only that the senses have a certain bias of their own which will modify every state in which they are called into play. There is a delight of the eye and ear, a pleasantness to the touch, an agreeableness of taste and smell, wholly without reference to anything beyond. The arts which employ any of these senses must satisfy their bias, however much they may appeal to higher faculties; nothing which rankly offends them can by any possible means be made beautiful. Thus painting must be charming in color, and music in tone; and certain colors and tones *are* charming for no deeper reason than that which makes certain foods palatable.

The interest in *perception* [3] assumes special prominence in the great visual art of painting. For the process of perception is most elaborated in connection with the sense of vision, this being peculiarly the human organ of watchfulness and orientation. The interest in perception is the interest in completing the sensation or rounding it into an object or situation with the aid of thought and imagination. In painting, as most commonly in life, the stimulus is visual—texture, perspective, or a quality of light.

The *emotional* form of apprehension plays the predominant part in representations of human action, in music, and in the appreciation of nature. It is in this latter connection that we can, I think, best understand it; and I propose for purposes of illustration to record an experience of my own.

I walked one night on the deck of a steamer plying between New York and Bermuda, and gave myself up wholly to the aspect of nature. The moon shone brightly half-way between the horizon and zenith, and opened a path of light from where I stood to the uttermost distance. With half-closed eyes I watched the hard lustre of the waves, or turned from this to the smooth roll of the foam turned up by the steamer's prow. And I remember that I seemed to dwell upon these things with an instant relish, like that with which my lungs devoured the fresh and plentiful air. But when I looked towards the moon along the path of light, there was something that stirred me more deeply. The prospect of an endless journey opened

CRITICISM OF FINE ART

out before me, like an invitation to live, or a fulness of opportunity. And I seemed to leap in response, rejoicing in my power. But I did not act; it was as though I already achieved and possessed. Presently I turned from the path of light to the blackness that beset it on every side. In this blackness there seemed to lurk every kind of unknown danger; I was moved with a sense of helplessness, and shrank from the thought of being deserted there. And yet though I was afraid, the fear never seemed to *possess me*, but always to be possessed *by* me, as mine to prolong and exult in as I would.

Now I think that the interpretation of my dream is this. Deeply implanted in the organism are certain co-ordinated responses such as courage and fear, or such as love, hate, combativeness, pity, and emulation. They may owe their present form to habit, but they are all rooted in instinct, and so call the body into play as a unit. Primarily they are plans of action, through which the organism promptly deals with practical emergencies. But it is possible for man to detach himself from overt motor relations with his environment; and in this case these responses return as it were into the body and reverberate there, taking on a purely emotional form which may be valued for itself. Thus courage and fear may lead to no act of bravery or caution, but remain simply *experiences* of courage and fear, promoted and treasured by the imagination. Nature will probably remain the object which evokes these responses most keenly, because nature is the hereditary environment towards which they were originally directed. But human action is scarcely less moving. Hence dramatic art, or the representation of social and moral confrontations, will both arouse and prolong the old passions, thus evoking a deeper and more massive response than the play of the senses.

I fully recognize that the value of dramatic art is by no means limited to its emotional appeal. I contend only that it does make such an appeal, and that it owes to that appeal, to its evoking of sympathy, love, or hate, to its stirring of incipient action, the peculiar intensity and reverberance of the enjoyment which it affords. The same holds true, I think, of poetry generally, where this deals with life. The case of music is more doubtful. It is generally agreed that the enjoyment of music has never been adequately accounted for, albeit it is probably more ancient than man. But that music does arouse the great emotions, and owe its popularity mainly to that fact, can scarcely be questioned. It is only necessary to add that over and above this appeal, as well as its appeal to the ear and to an intellectual apprehension of its technical forms, it seems to

CRITICISM OF FINE ART

be capable of developing emotions of its own; that is, experiences which do not coincide with the instinctive emotions, but which have a like massiveness and organic reverberation. It may be, as Walter Pater insists, that in this respect "all art constantly aspires towards the condition of music."[5] But this does not contradict the fact that such arts *are* emotionally stimulating, will always stir men as men are capable of being stirred, and in society at large will make their main appeal to the fundamental and constant emotions, cultivating the enjoyment of love, fear, and the other elemental passions for the very poignancy and thrill of them.

For the intellectual type of apprehension I propose to employ the term *discernment*. I mean the apprehension of an *idea* when conveyed by some sensuous medium; the finding or recovery of some unity of thought in a perceptual context. When discernment in this sense is directly agreeable without any ulterior motive, it is a special case of the æsthetic interest. From this interest the representative or pictorial element in art derives its value.

Let me illustrate my meaning by referring to what Taine says of Greek sculpture:

Here we have the living body, complete and without a veil, admired and glorified, standing on its pedestal without scandal and exposed to all eyes.

What is its purpose, and what idea, through sympathy, is the statue to convey to spectators? An idea which, to us, is almost without meaning because it belongs to another age and another epoch of the human mind. The head is without significance; unlike ours it is not a world of graduated conceptions, excited passions, and a medley of sentiments; the face is not sunken, sharp, and disturbed; it has not many characteristics, scarcely any expression, and is generally in repose. . . . The contemporaries of Pericles and Plato did not require violent and surprising effects to stimulate weary attention or to irritate an uneasy sensibility. A blooming and healthy body, capable of all virile and gymnastic actions, a man or woman of fine growth and noble race, a serene form in full light, a simple and natural harmony of lines happily commingled, was the most animated spectacle they could dwell on. They desired to contemplate man proportioned to his organs and to his condition and endowed with every perfection within these limits; they demanded nothing more and nothing less; anything besides would have struck them as extravagance, deformity, or disease. Such is the circle within which the simplicity of their culture kept them.[6]

In other words, Greek art expressed the rare quality of Greek life; its naturalism, its compactness, its clearness. And it did so instinctively both to the artist and the spectator. We are not to think that because, in order to understand ancient art, it may be necessary for us first to obtain a conception of life and then to match it in art, this is essential to its appreciation. On the contrary, the object of art is not beautiful until it flashes the idea upon us, communicating an ideal unity that is not intellectually articulate at all. This must always be the effect upon contemporaries, in whom the idea is so assimilated as to be unconscious. But the idea is there none the less; and the full beauty cannot exist for any one who is incapable of discerning the idea, and rejoicing in the apprehension of it.

The incomparable excellence of Greek sculpture is due to a type of genius in which clearness of mind and delicacy of touch are united. Among the Greeks the term infinite was a term of disparagement; they thought roundly and cleanly, thus preferring ideas to vague surmises. This was their first gift. And, adding to it a sensitiveness to form, they were enabled to *express themselves*, without redundancy and exaggeration, bringing whatever medium they employed into accord with the idea. It is this felicity and luminousness that gives to the art of the Greeks a peculiar appeal to the intelligence. For the mind delights in definiteness and light.

But the Greek conception of life belongs to an age preceding the advent of what has proved to be the European religion. And Christianity has so reconstructed the experience of the average man through its sensitiveness to pain, and its emphasis on what is called "the inner life," that I want further to illustrate the meaning of discernment in art, by referring to the representation of the spirit of the Renaissance in the painting of Leonardo da Vinci. I quote the following from Pater's description of "La Gioconda":

> The presence that thus rose so strangely beside the waters, is expressive of what in the ways of a thousand years men had come to desire. Hers is the head upon which all "the ends of the world are come," and the eyelids are a little weary. It is a beauty wrought out from within upon the flesh, the deposit, little cell by cell, of strange thoughts and fantastic reveries and exquisite passions. Set it for a moment beside one of those white Greek goddesses or beautiful women of antiquity, and how would they be troubled by this beauty, into which the soul with all its maladies has passed. All the thoughts and experience of the world have etched and moulded there, in that which they have of power to refine and make expressive the human form, the animalism of Greece, the lust of Rome, the reveries of the middle age with its spiritual ambition and imaginative loves, the return of the pagan world, the sins of the Borgias. She is older than the rocks among which she sits; like the vampire, which has been dead many times, and learned the secrets of the grave; and has been a diver in deep seas, and keeps their fallen day about her; and trafficked for strange webs with Eastern merchants; and, as Leda, was the mother of Helen of Troy, and, as Saint Anne, the mother of Mary; and all this has been to her but as the sound of lyres and flutes, and lives only in the delicacy with which it has moulded the changing lineaments, and tinged the eyelids and the hands.[7]

The power of Renaissance painting is not wholly a matter of color, texture, modelling, and composition; for though it contains these and many sensuous and perceptual values besides, it conveys through them with surpassing truth and delicacy ideas as evasive as they are subtle and profound. There is an ecstasy of mind in the discernment of these ideas, and a blend of emotion that follows in their train, both of which are conditioned by insight; that is, by a process that is neither sensuous, perceptual, nor emotional merely, but, in an additional sense, intellectual.

The interest in apprehension may thus be exhibited and satisfied in divers ways, differing according to the special processes of consciousness which they call into play. And while it may be crude or cultivated, it is safe to say that in all of its modes it is present to some degree in every individual human life. The simple-minded person who hisses the villain of the melodrama, and he who takes pleasure in the inevitableness of the Greek tragedy, are exhibiting the same interest in the emotions evoked by the spectacle of life. There is only a difference of training and sophistication between the man who enjoys a cheap chromo for the color or the "likeness," and one who appreciates Velasquez's treatment of light or the characterization of Franz Hals.

In the enjoyment of the highest forms of art these various modes of apprehension will be united, each so contributing to the enhancement of the rest that it is impossible sharply to divide them. Nor do I venture any opinion as to which of these modes, if any, is fundamental in the different arts or in fine art as a whole. It is sufficient for our purposes to know that art does exercise and develop human nature in all of these ways.

We are now in a position to define a programme of criticism. Art thrives because it fulfils a complex and multiform interest. It is supported by an interest which it supplies with its proper objects. Hence it falls within the circle of life where questions of prudence, justice, and good-will are paramount. But, because moral considerations must thus in the nature of the case take precedence over purely æsthetic considerations, this proves nothing whatsoever concerning the way in which this precedence should be established. It was Plato's belief that society should employ a rigorous censorship, and banish the offending poet:

> We will fall down and worship him as a sweet and holy and wonderful being; but we must also inform him that there is no place for such as he is in our State—the law will not allow them. And so when we have anointed him with myrrh, and set a garland of wool upon his head, we shall send him away to another city.[8]

But there is another way of protecting society from whatever may be the evil effects of art, and that is to educate the individual and the community in their use of art. This would mean, in place of a regulation of the supply, a regulation of the demand. It would mean that the æsthetic interest itself, like every other interest within the moral economy, should be so controlled as to make it as conducive as possible to health and abundance of life. The exercise or cultivation of the interest in art would then, like the love of nature or of social intercourse, be unlimited so far as its objects were concerned, but limited through its relation to other interests within the individual or community purpose. But with this difference concerning the proper remedy, the present inquiry will coincide in its intent and presuppositions with that model of all moral criticisms, the *Republic* of Plato. What are the possibilities for life of this æsthetic interest or love of art? How is it liable to abuse or excess? What is its bearing on other interests, and how far does it tend to make life gracious and happy, without destroying its balance or compromising its truth? These are the questions on which I hope that I may be able to throw some light by calling attention to the following characteristics possessed by the æsthetic interest: *self-sufficiency, pervasiveness, vicariousness, stimulation of action, fixation of ideas*, and *liberality*.[9]

III

It has long been pointed out that the æsthetic interest, unlike the bodily appetites, is *self-sufficient*, in that it is capable of being evenly sustained. It depends on no antecedent craving, and has no definite periodic limit of satiety. It engages the capacities that are, on the whole, the most docile and the least liable to progressive fatigue, while through its own internal variety it is guarded against monotony. Consequently the æsthetic interest is peculiarly capable of being continued and developed through a lifetime, providing a constant and increasing source of satisfaction.

Furthermore, the æsthetic interest is resourceful, easily supplying itself with the objects which it uses. It follows that it contributes to independence, being like the "speculative activity" of Aristotle, [10] in giving the individual a means of happiness in himself without the aid of his fellows or the favor of fortune. Since the æsthetic interest is in these ways self-sufficient, its continuous return of good being guaranteed, it is one of the safest of investments.

But every special interest is a source of danger in direct proportion to its isolation. Its very self-sufficiency may serve to promote a narrow concentration, a blindness to ulterior interests and wider possibilities. This undue dwelling on the given material of life may, as we have seen in an earlier chapter, attach to any interest; but the æsthetic interest is peculiarly liable to it. This is due to the fact that, in so far as an object appeals to the æsthetic interest, it tends not to develop, but to retain some fixed aspect in which the apprehension of it is agreeable. The various practical interests ramify indefinitely through the dynamic relations of objects, and through the handling of objects common to a variety of interests. Once engaged in what is called "active life" one tends to be drawn into the main current of enterprise and made aware of the larger issues. And the theoretical interest also tends to lead beyond itself; for it prompts the mind to examine the whole nature of objects, and to explore their context without limit in the hope of completer truth. But the æsthetic interest readily acquires equilibrium, and feels no inducement to leave off an activity which, though its limits may be narrow, is free and continuous within them. Plato accused art of being essentially imitative, and so of confirming the vulgar respect for the surface aspect of things.[11] It is truer, I think, to say that the æsthetic interest is quiescent, tending to perpetuate experience in any form that is found pleasant, and without respect either to practical exigencies or to the order of truth.

Hence this interest on account of its very self-sufficiency offers a passive resistance to the formal principles of moral organization—to prudence, purpose, justice, and good-will.

IV

The æsthetic interest is the good genius of the powers of apprehension, making them fruitful in their own kind. Now the powers of apprehension are engaged during all the waking hours, and if they can be taught to mediate a good of their own, that good will *pervade* the whole of life. It is through the cultivation of the æsthetic interest that there is most hope of redeeming the waste places, of giving to intervals and accidental juxtapositions some graciousness and profit. With all the world to see and contemplate, and with the eye and mind wherewith to contemplate them, there is a limitless abundance of good things always and everywhere available. Let me quote Arthur Benson's account of this discovery:

The world was full of surprises; trees drooped their leaves over screening walls, houses had backs as well as fronts; music was heard from shuttered windows, lights burned in upper rooms. There were a thousand pretty secrets in the ways of people to each other. Then, too, there were ideas, as thick as sparrows in an ivied wall. One had but to clap one's hands and cry out, and there was a fluttering of innumerable wings; life was as full of bubbles, forming, rising into amber foam, as a glass of sparkling wine.[12]

To this delight which the casual environment affords a sensitive observer, art may add through a decorous furnishing of city and house. Or the instruments of other interests may be made to give pleasure of themselves, so that there may be no long periods of deferred reward. Thus to the hire of manual labor may be added the immediate compensation which comes from a love of the tools, or from the satisfaction taken in the aspect of work done; to physical exercise may be added the love of nature, to scholarship the love of scientific form, and to social intercourse the love of personal beauty or of conversation. In these ways, and in countless ways beside, the æsthetic interest may multiply the richness of life.

Society is, on the whole, protected against the danger of overemphasis on the æsthetic interest, through the habitual subordination of it in public opinion to standards of efficiency. Men commonly believe, and are justified in so believing, that a life delivered wholly to the æsthetic interest is frivolous; amusing itself with "bubbles" and "amber foam," while supported by a community in whose graver and more urgent concerns it takes no part. Probably no one has done more than Pater to persuade men of the present generation that it is worth while to "catch at any exquisite passion, . . . or any stirring of the senses"; and yet he is not a prophet in our day. Is it possibly because in that same famous conclusion to the *Renaissance* he said, "Not the fruit of experience, but experience itself, is the end," [13] and thus exposed himself to misunderstanding, if not to refutation, at the hands of any one of average moral enlightenment? The moral lesson is one that none have escaped, and that only a few are permitted to forget. This lesson has taught with unvarying reiteration that acts are to be judged by their consequences; that all purposes are constructive, and so far as wise fitted into the building of civilization; that experience itself, in Pater's sense, is possible only as a fruit of experience. A life in which the æsthetic interest unduly dominates, in which action is transmuted into pulses of sensation, and the means of efficiency into the ends of contemplation, is an idle life, protected from the consequences of its own impotency only by the constructive labor of others. He who from prolonged gazing at the spoon forgets to carry it to his mouth, must die of hunger and cease from gazing altogether, or be fed by his friends. The instruments of achievement may be adorned, and made delightful in the using, but they must not on that account be mistaken for the achievement; leisure may be made a worthy pastime through the cultivation of the sensibilities, but it must not be substituted for vocation, or allowed to infect a serious purpose with decay.

V

It has always been recognized that there is a peculiar massiveness or depth in æsthetic satisfaction, as though it somehow carried with it the satisfaction of all interests. And this is not due merely to the fact that other interests tend to fall away or remit their claims; it is due besides to the fact that other interests may in a sense actually be fulfilled in the æsthetic interest. In other words, this interest serves a *vicarious* function, transmuting other interests into its own form, and then affording them a fulfilment which they are incapable of attaining when exercised in their own right.

This occurs when other interests, such as love or personal ambition, are imagined or represented, and thus made objects of agreeable apprehension. There is in this a compensation for failure, without which life would be stripped of one of its main barriers against despair. Those whom circumstance has provided no opportunity for the fulfilment of interests so ingenerate as maternal love or heroic action, may, in a way, make themselves whole through the contemplation of these things; for the contemplation of them engages the same instincts, arouses the same emotions, but without requiring the existence of their objects. The prolongation of arduous and uncertain effort is compensated through the imaginative anticipation of success, or through the apprehension of some symbol of perfect fruition. It is through this happy illumination of struggle with a vision of fulfilment, that mankind is reconciled to such tasks as civilization and spiritual wholeness; tasks in which great efforts produce small results, and of which the end is not seen.

Now it remains true, of course, that such vicarious fulfilment is not real fulfilment; and to suppose it to be, is one of the most serious errors for which the æsthetic interest is responsible. The man who, with clenched hands and quickened pulse, is watching some image of himself as it triumphs over obstacles and arrives at the summit of his ambition, may and doubtless does *feel* like Alexander, but he nevertheless has not conquered the world; and if he thinks he has, he will probably never conquer any of it. It must be remembered that the vicarious æsthetic fulfilment of interests is the easiest fulfilment of them; and that it may, therefore, become a form of self-indulgence and a source of false complacency. A sanguine imagination is one of the

CRITICISM OF FINE ART 199

chief causes of worldly failure; an exaggerated interest in representations of virtue is a common cause of irresponsibility and of hypocrisy. William James, in a passage that is frequently quoted, calls attention also to the danger of acquiring a chronic emotionality.

> The weeping of a Russian lady over the fictitious personages in the play, while her coachman is freezing to death on his seat outside, is the sort of thing that everywhere happens on a less glaring scale. Even the habit of excessive indulgence in music, for those who are neither performers themselves nor musically gifted enough to take it in a purely intellectual way, has probably a relaxing effect upon the character. One becomes filled with emotions which habitually pass without prompting to any deed, and so the inertly sentimental condition is kept up. The remedy would be, never to suffer one's self to have an emotion at a concert, without expressing it afterwards in *some* active way. Let the expression be the least thing in the world—speaking genially to one's aunt, or giving up one's seat in a horse-car, if nothing more heroic offers—but let it not fail to take place.[14]

But not only is it possible through the exaggeration of the æsthetic interest to substitute apparent achievement for real achievement; it is possible to extract solace from the contemplation of failure itself. Is there any one who has not met the man who is actually made buoyant by his consistent misfortune? For it is flattering that an evil fate should single one out from the crowd for conspicuous attention, that all the tragedy of existence should centre upon one's devoted head. And a certain interest attaches even to unredeemed misery and abject futility on their own account, if only they can be viewed from the right angle, and with a cultivated sense for such things. Now thus to poetize the tragedy of one's own life is fatuous; it is like enjoying one's dizziness on the brink of a precipice, or the pangs of sickness without seeking a remedy. But to poetize the tragedy of others, to fiddle while Rome is burning, is brutal. Nevertheless, though it is not commonly possible to do things on Nero's scale, precisely the same attitude is the commonest thing in the world, and is fostered by the whole æsthetic bias of the race. The meanness of savage life, the squalid poverty of the slums, suffice in their picturesqueness to make a holiday for those who are more occupied with images than with deeds. And there is actually a philosophy of life in which all things are held to be good because they afford a tragic, sublime, and, therefore, pleasing spectacle. This is the very extreme of moral infidelity, the abandonment of the will to make good for the insidious and relaxing interest in making things seem good as they are.

VI

That a beautiful object commonly *stimulates* a motor response is beyond question. Even when it does not appeal to any definite emotion it is *generally* stimulating, through its affording to the natural powers at some point an unusual harmony with their environment. And when there is a definite emotional appeal, there is a tendency to act. For, as we have seen, originally the fundamental emotions were all co-ordinated reactions to the environment, enlisting the whole organism to cope with some practical emergency. That the emotions should become *mere* emotions is due to the modification of instinct by habit. Whatever, then, arouses the emotions does in some degree stir to action. So that one of the most important moral uses of art is its alliance with other interests in order to intensify their appeal, in order to make them more instantly moving. Art is a means of enlivening dormant impulses; as music is a means of rekindling the love of country or the love of God, so that men may be brought to take up arms with enthusiasm or endure reverses without complaint.

But this motor excitement which art stimulates may be morally indeterminate; that is, it may be capable of being discharged in any way that accident or bias may select. In other words, art may communicate power without controlling its use, thus merely increasing the disorder and instability of life. Or it may serve to exaggerate the appeal of the present interest, until it becomes ungovernable and obscures ulterior interests. This tendency to promote dissoluteness is the most serious charge which Plato brings against the arts. After referring to the unseemly hilarity to which men are incited by the comic stage, he adds:

And the same may be said of lust and anger and all the other affections, of desire and pain and pleasure which are held to be inseparable from every action—in all of them poetry feeds and waters the passions instead of drying them up; she lets them rule instead of ruling them as they ought to be ruled, with a view to the happiness and virtue of mankind.[15]

In an earlier passage Plato discusses types of music in relation to action, the Lydian which is sorrowful, and the Ionian which is indolent; showing that selection must be made if men are not to be at the mercy of random influences. It is not necessary, as Plato would have it, to banish Lydian and Ionian harmonies from society; but within one's personal economy, within the republic of one's own soul, one must prefer with Plato those stirrings of the emotions which support and re-enforce one's moral purpose:

Of the harmonies I know nothing, but I want to have one warlike, which will sound the word or note which a brave man utters in the hour of danger and stern resolve, or when his cause is failing, and he is going to wounds or death or is overtaken by some other evil, and at every such crisis meets fortune with calmness and endurance; and another to be used by him in times of peace and freedom of action, when there is no pressure of necessity, and he is seeking to persuade God by prayer, or man by instruction and advice. . . . These two harmonies I ask you to leave: the strain of necessity and the strain of freedom, the strain of the unfortunate and the strain of the fortunate, the strain of courage and the strain of temperance; these, I say, leave.[16]

VII

Where art is not employed directly to incite action, it may still be indirectly conducive to action through *fixing* ideas and inclining the sentiments towards them. This is probably its most important moral function. The ideas which are of the greatest significance for conduct are ideas which receive no adequate embodiment in the objects of nature. Every broad purpose and developed ideal requires the exercise of the constructive imagination. But the immediate images of the imagination are fluctuating and transient, and need to be supported through being embodied in some enduring medium. Thus monuments serve as emblems of nationality; or, as in the thirteenth century, all the arts may unite to represent and suggest the objects of religious faith. Poetry and song have always served as means of incarnating the more delicate shadings of a racial ideal; and every man would be a poet if he could, and trace the outline of that hope which stirs him and which is not the hope of any other man.

But it must be made clear that art does more than make ideas definite and permanent. It inclines the sentiments towards them. The great power of art lies in its function of making ideas alluring. Now whatever is loved or admired is, in the long run, sought out, imitated, and served. Understanding this, the ancient Athenians sought to educate the passions, and employed music to that end. This is Aristotle's justification of such a course:

> Since then music is a pleasure, and virtue consists in rejoicing and loving and hating aright, there is clearly nothing which we are so much concerned to acquire and to cultivate as the power of forming right judgments, and of taking delight in good dispositions and noble actions. Rhythm and melody supply imitations of anger and gentleness, and also of courage and temperance and of virtues and vices in general, which hardly fall short of the actual affections, as we know from our own experience, for in listening to such strains our souls undergo a change. The habit of feeling pleasure or pain at mere representations is not far removed from the same feeling about realities.[17]

The simple and incontestable truth of these statements is a standing condemnation of the usual environment of youth. Virtue consists, as much as it ever did, "in rejoicing and loving and hating aright"; but the guidance of these sentiments to their proper objects is left almost wholly to chance. It is by making the good also beautiful, by illuminating the modes of virtue with jewels, and endearing them to the imagination, that the moral reason may be re-enforced from early days by high spirits. It should be a task of education, using this means either in the home or the school or the city at large, to inculcate a right habit of admiration.

If art is to serve a moral end in fixing and embellishing ideas, it must be *true*. What I mean by this most important qualification I must now endeavor to make plain. Art, in so far as it is a means of representation, deals either with physical nature, as in landscape and figure painting, or with types and incidents of human life, as in dramatic painting and in the greater part of poetry. In either case it may, like thought, either reflect or distort the structure of reality. Now the real structure of human life is moral; consisting only in a variety of instances of the one law that *the wages of sin is death*. To represent life otherwise is to falsify it, precisely as to represent bodies without solidity and gravity is to falsify physical nature. But in representing physical nature art does not, as science does, formulate merely its geometrical or dynamical skeleton; to do so would be contrary to the intent of art to represent things in their perceptual concreteness. Similarly art does not represent abstract virtues. Nevertheless, if it is not to depart from the truth art must, at the same time that it conveys the color and vividness of life, also conform to its proper laws, and demonstrate the consequences of action as they are. And the same standard of clearness and fidelity, which requires that great art shall reveal nature as it is, not to the superficial or imitative observer but to the thoughtful and penetrating mind, requires also that it shall throw into relief the profounder and more universal forces of life.

Great art, therefore, is of necessity enlightening. But it is possible that untruth should parade in the dress and under the auspices of art, and so work to the confusion of the moral consciousness. If art were only realistic in the full sense, an unequivocal representation of the laws of life, it would invariably justify and support the moral will; it would be idealistic. It is the art of desultory and irresponsible fancy that is a source of danger. There is a species of romantic art that is guarded by its very excess of fantasy; it being impossible to mistake it for a representation of life. But where romantic art is not thus clear in its motive, it becomes what is called "sensational" art, in which the wages of sin are not paid; in which imprudence, infidelity, and a mean ambition are made to yield success, freedom, and glorious achievement. The realities are violated, with the consequence that resolve is weakened and the intelligence bewildered.

Since art may be true or untrue, it may also be universal or particular, profound or superficial, in its apprehension of reality. This difference has operated to define a scale of importance in art, so far as the interest of society is concerned. There is at least a measure of truth in Taine's graduated scale by which he estimates the greatness of art according as it represents the fashion of the day, the type of the generation, the type of the age, the type of the race, or man himself in his immutable nature.[18] That art will be the most effective instrument of moral enlightenment which reflects the experience of mankind in the basal and constant virtues, giving quality and distinction to truths which might otherwise suffer from their very homeliness and familiarity.

There is a kindred consideration to which Tolstóy, undiscerning as he is in most of his criticism of art, has very justly called attention. In the broad sense, art is liable to untruth from reflecting exclusively the bias of a certain temperament. The following description of a class of contemporary dramas is not wholly inapt:

> They either represent an architect, who for some reason has not fulfilled his former high resolves and in consequence of this climbs on the roof of a house built by him and from there flies down headlong; or some incomprehensible old woman, who raises rats and for some unknown reason takes a poetic child to the sea and there drowns it; or some blind people, who, sitting at the sea-shore, for some reason all the time repeat one and the same thing; or a bell which flies into a lake and there keeps ringing.[19]

That a tendency to cultivate acquaintance with the curious and rare, and communicate it to a narrow group of initiated persons, is characteristic of modern times, and that on the whole it is a symptom of decadence, Tolstóy has, I believe, proved. At any rate, the effect of such a tendency in art can not fail to be morally injurious, since life is not represented proportionately. Art has much to do with the vogue and prestige of ideas. Thus, for example, though the problem-play may be faithful to life where it deals with life, if the stage be given over wholly to this form of drama, there will almost inevitably result a false conception of the degree to which the incidents selected are representative of social conditions on the whole.

There is one further source of moral error in connection with this function of art. Because art can not only fix ideas but also make them alluring, it may invest them with a fictitious value. I refer to what is only a different aspect of that sentimentalism or chronic emotionalism to which I have already called attention. Not only is it possible that men should be brought through the æsthetic interest to replace action with emotion; they may also persuade themselves that the higher principles of life owe their validity to some quality that is discerned immediately in the apprehension of them. But purpose, justice, and goodwill are essentially principles of organization; their virtue is their provident working. To regard them only as images with a value inhering in their bare essence, is to forfeit their benefits. Verbalism, formalism, mysticism, are given a certain false charm and semblance of self-sufficiency by the cultivation and exercise of the æsthetic interest. Hence morality and religion must here resist its enticements, and never cease to remind themselves that theirs is the task of acknowledging all interests according to their real inwardness, and of banishing cruelty and blindness in their behalf.

VIII

Finally, art serves to *liberalize* life, to make it expansive and generous in spirit. This is possible because, in the first place, art is unworldly. I mean simply that the enjoyment of beauty is not a part of ambition; that it does not call into play those habits of calculation and forms of skill that conduce to success in livelihood or the gaining of any of the proximate ends of organized social life. It frees the mind from its harness and turns it out to pasture. I suppose that every one has had that experience of spiritual refreshment which occasionally comes when one has gone body and soul *out of doors*, or when one is delivered over to the enchantment of sober and elevating music, and suddenly made aware of the better things that have been long forgotten. Such experiences are a moral inspiration. It is as though, the clamor of the world being for the moment shut out, one hears at last the voices that speak with authority. For an instant the broad sweep of truth flashes upon eyes that have been too intently watchful of affairs near at hand. The good-will can be sustained only by a mind that now and then withdraws itself from its engagements, and expands its view to the full measure of life. For the momentary inhibiting of the narrower practical impulses, and the evoking of this quiet and contemplative mood, the love of nature and the love of art are the most reliable means.

But art promotes liberality of spirit in an even more definitely moral sense. For art, like all forms of culture, and like the service of humanity,

CRITICISM OF FINE ART

provides for the highest type of social intercourse. The æsthetic interest is one of those rare interests which are common to all men without being competitive. All men require bread, but since this interest requires exclusive possession of its objects, its very commonness is a source of suspicion and enmity. Similarly all men require truth and beauty and civilization, but these objects are enhanced by the fact that all may rejoice in them without their being divided or becoming the property of any man. They bring men together without rivalry and intrigue, in a spirit of good-fellowship. "Culture," says Matthew Arnold, "is not satisfied till we *all* come to a perfect man; it knows that the sweetness and light of the few must be imperfect until the raw and unkindled masses of humanity are touched with sweetness and light."

'This,' he continues, 'is the *social idea;* and the men of culture are the true apostles of equality. The great men of culture are those who have had a passion for diffusing, for making prevail, for carrying from one end of society to the other, the best knowledge, the best ideas of their time; who have labored to divest knowledge of all that was harsh, uncouth, difficult, abstract, professional, exclusive; to humanize it, to make it efficient outside the clique of the cultivated and learned, yet still remaining the *best* knowledge and thought of the time, and a true source, therefore, of sweetness and light.'[20]

Art, both in the creation and in the enjoyment of it, is thus true to the deepest motive of morality. It is a remoulding of nature to the end that all may live, and that they may live abundantly.

IX

I have sought to place before you what art may contribute to life. It will have become plain that while art is the natural and powerful ally of morality, it does not itself provide any guarantee of proper control; in the interests of goodness, on the whole, no man can surrender himself to it utterly. The good-will is not proved until, as Plato said, it is *tried with enchantments,* and found to be strong and true. Goodness can not be cast upon a man like a spell; it is a work of rational organization, and can not be had without discipline, efficiency, and service. But it is for art to surround life with fit auspices; to create an environment that reflects and forecasts its best achievements, thus both making a home for it and confirming its resolves.

Having modelled this moral criticism of art upon the method of Plato, I shall conclude with his familiar summary of all the wisdom and eloquence that there is in the matter:

Let our artists rather be those who are gifted to discern the true nature of beauty and grace; then will our youth dwell in the land of health, amid fair sights and sounds; and beauty, the effluence of fair works, will visit the eye and ear, like a healthful breeze from a purer region, and insensibly draw the soul even in childhood into harmony with the beauty of reason.[21]

CHAPTER VI

THE MORAL JUSTIFICATION OF RELIGION [1]

I

It is generally agreed that religion is either the paramount issue or the most serious obstacle to progress. To its devotees religion is of overwhelming importance; to unbelievers it is, in the phrasing of Burke, "superstitious folly, enthusiastical nonsense, and holy tyranny." The difference between the friends and the enemies of religion may, I think, be resolved as follows:

Religion recognizes some final arbitration of human destiny; it is a lively awareness of the fact that, while man proposes, it is only within certain narrow limits that he can dispose his own plans. His nicest adjustments and most ardent longings are overruled; he knows that until he can discount or conciliate that which commands his fortunes his condition is precarious and miserable. And through his eagerness to save himself he leaps to conclusions that are uncritical and premature. Irreligion, on the other hand, flourishes among those who are more snugly intrenched

JUSTIFICATION OF RELIGION 215

within the cities of man. It is a product of civilization. Comfortably housed as he is, and enjoying an artificial illumination behind drawn blinds, the irreligious man has the heart to criticise the hasty speculations and abject fear of those who stand without in the presence of the surrounding darkness. In other words, religion is perpetually on the exposed side of civilization, sensitive to the blasts that blow from the surrounding universe; while irreligion is in the lee of civilization, with enough remove from danger to foster a refined concern for logic and personal liberty. There is a sense, then, in which both religion and irreligion are to be justified. If religion is guilty of unreason, irreligion is guilty of apathy. For without doubt the situation of the individual man is broadly such as religion conceives it to be. There is nothing that he can build, nor any precaution that he can take, that weighs appreciably in the balance against the powers which decree good and ill fortune, catastrophe and triumph, life and death. Hence to be without fear is the part of folly. Behold, the fear of the Lord, that is wisdom.

Religion is man's recognition of the overruling control of his fortunes. It is neither metaphysical nor mythical, but urgently practical. Primeval chaos, Chronos, the father of Zeus, and the long line of speculative Absolutes have no worshippers because they take no hand in man's affairs. They may be neglected with impunity. But not so the gods who send health and sickness, fertility and death, victory and defeat; or He who sits in judgment on the last day to determine the doom of eternity. Religion is the manifestation of supreme concern for life, an alertness to the remotest threat of danger and promise of hope. A certain momentousness attaches to all the affairs of religion, because everything is at stake. Its dealings are with the last court of appeal, in behalf of the most indispensable good.

In form, religion is a case of *belief;* that is, of settled conviction. There is no religion until some interpretation of life, some accommodation between man and God, has been so far accepted as to be unhesitatingly practised. The absurdity of doubt in matters of religion has been pointed out in the well-known parody, "O God, if there be a God, save my soul, if I have a soul." The quality of religion lies not in the entertaining of a speculative hypothesis, but in an assurance so confident that its object is not only thought but enacted. God is not God until his unquestioned existence is assimilated to life. Indeed, it is conceivable that an object thus made the basis of action should still remain theoretically doubtful. To Fontenelle is attributed the remark that he "did not believe in ghosts, but was afraid of

JUSTIFICATION OF RELIGION

them." This is a paradox until we distinguish theoretical and practical conviction; then it becomes not only credible but commonplace. If one prays to God, it is not necessary for the purposes of religion that one should, in Fontenelle's sense, believe in him. But I prefer to use the term "belief" more strictly, to connote such assent as expresses itself, not in a deliberate judgment made conformable to one's intellectual conscience, but in fear, love, and purpose, in habitual imagery, in any attitude or activity that spontaneously and freely presupposes the object with which it deals.

By conceiving religion as belief we may understand not only its air of certainty, but also the variety of its forms and agencies. Belief sits at the centre of life and qualifies all its manifestations. Hence the futility of attempting to associate religion exclusively with any single function of man. The guises in which religious belief may appear are as multiform as human nature, and will vary with every shading of mood and temperament. Its central objects may be thought, imagined, or dealt with—in short, responded to in all the divers ways, internal and overt, that the powers and occasions of life define.

This will suffice, I trust, to lay the general topic of religion before us. I shall employ the terms and phrases which I have formulated as a working definition: *Religion is belief on the part of individuals or communities concerning the final or overruling control of their interests.*[2] I propose from this point to keep in the forefront of the discussion the standards whereby religion is to be estimated, and approved or condemned. On what grounds may a religion be criticised? What would constitute the proof of an absolute religion? History is strewn with discredited religions; men began to quarrel over religion so soon as they had any; and it is customary for every religious devotee to believe jealously and exclusively. There can be no doubt, then, that religion is subject to justification; it remains to distinguish the tests which may with propriety be applied, and in particular to isolate and emphasize the moral test.

II

In the first place, let me mention briefly a test which it is customary to apply, but which is not so much an estimate as it is a measure. I refer to the various respects in which an individual or community may be said to be *more* or *less* religious. Thus, for example, certain religious phenomena surpass others in acuteness or intensity. This is peculiarly true of the phenomena manifested in conversion and in revivals. In this respect the mysteries of the ancients exceeded

JUSTIFICATION OF RELIGION

their regular public worship. Individuals and communities vary in the degree to which they are capable of enthusiasm, excitement, or ecstasy.

Or a religion may be measured extensively. He whose religion is constant and uniform is more religious than he whose observance is confined to the Sabbath day, or he whose concern in the matter appears only in time of trouble or at the approach of death. This test may best be summed up in terms of consistency. Religion may vary in the degree to which it pervades the various activities of life. That religion is confined and small which manifests itself only in words or public deeds or emotions exclusively. If it is to be effective it must be systematic, so thoroughly adopted as to be cumulative and progressive. It must engage every activity, qualify all thought and imagination, in short, infuse the whole of life with its saving grace.

It is clear, however, that a measure of religion does not constitute either proof or disproof. If a religion be good or true, or on like grounds accredited, then the more of it the better. But differences of degree appear in all religions. Indeed, the quantitative test has been most adequately met by forms of religion the warrant of which is generally held to be highly questionable. We may, therefore, dismiss this test without further consideration. The application of it must be based upon a prior and more fundamental justification.

There is one test of religion which has been universally applied by believers and critics alike, a test which, I think, will shortly appear to deserve precedence over all others. I refer to the test of truth. Every religion has been justified to its believers and recommended to unbelievers on grounds of evidence. It has been verified in its working, or attested by either observation, reflection, revelation, or authority.

In spite of the general assent which this proposition will doubtless command, 't is deserving of special emphasis at the present time. Students of religion have latterly shifted attention from its claims to truth to its utility and subjective form. This pragmatic and psychological study of religion has created no little confusion of mind concerning its real meaning, and obscured that which is after all its essential claim—the claim, namely, to offer an illumination of life. Religious belief, like all belief, is reducible to judgments. These judgments are not, it is true, explicit and theoretically formulated; but they are none the less answerable to evidence from that context of experience to which they refer. It is true that the believer's assurance is not consciously rational, but it is none the less liable before the court of reason. Cardinal Newman

JUSTIFICATION OF RELIGION

fairly expressed the difference between the method of religion and the method of science when he said that "ten thousand difficulties do not make one doubt," that "difficulty and doubt are incommensurate."[3] Nevertheless, the difficulties are in each case germane; and the fact that every article of faith has its besetting doubt is proof that the thorough justification of faith requires the settlement of theoretical difficulties.

No religion can survive the demonstration of its untruth; for salvation, whether present or eternal, depends on processes actually operative in the environment. Religion must reveal the undeniable situation and prepare man for it. It must charge the unbeliever with being guilty of folly, with deceiving himself through failing to see and take heed. Every religious propaganda is a cry of warning, putting men on their guard against invisible dangers; or a promise of succor, bringing glad tidings of great joy. And its prophecy is empty and trivial if the danger or the succor can be shown to be unreal. The one unfailing bias in life is the bias for disillusionment, springing from the organic instinct for that real environment to which, whether friendly or hostile, it must adapt itself. Every man knows in his heart that he can not be saved through being deceived. Illusions can not endure, and those who lightly perpetrate them are fortunate if they escape the resentment and swift vengeance which overtook the prophets of Baal.

The grounds of religious truth will require prolonged consideration; but before discussing them further let me first mention a test of religion which belongs to the class of psychological and pragmatic tests to which I have just alluded, but which has latterly assumed special prominence. Though realizing that I use a somewhat disparaging term, I suggest that we call this the "therapeutic test." It has been proved that the state of piety possesses a direct curative value through its capacity to exhilarate or pacify, according to the needs of a disordered mind. As a potent form of suggestion, it lends itself to the uses of psychiatry; it may be medicinally employed as a tonic, stimulant, or sedative.

Now we can afford to remind ourselves that, at least from the point of view of the patient, this use of religion bears a striking resemblance to certain primitive practices in which God was conceived as a glorified medicine-man, and the healing of the body strangely confused with spiritual regeneration. Bishop Gregory of Tours once addressed the following apostrophe to the worshipful St. Martin: "O unspeakable theriac! ineffable pigment! admirable antidote! celestial purgative! superior to all the skill of physicians, more fragrant than aromatic drugs, stronger than

JUSTIFICATION OF RELIGION

all ointments combined! thou cleanest the bowels as well as scammony, and the lungs as well as hyssop; thou cleanest the head as well as camomile!" [4]

It is true that religion is in these days recommended for more subtle disorders; but even religious ecstasy may be virtually equivalent to a mere state of emotional exhilaration, or piety to a condition of mental and moral stupor. What does it profit a man to be content with his lot, or to experience the rapture of the saints, if he has lost his soul? The saving of a soul is a much more serious matter than the cessation of worry or the curing of insomnia, or even than the acquiring of a habit of delirious joy. Tranquillity and happiness are, it is true, the legitimate fruits of religion, but only provided they be infused with goodness and truth. If religion is to be a spiritual tonic, and not merely a physical tonic, it must be based on moral organization and intellectual enlightenment. I do not doubt that religion has in all times recommended itself to men mainly through its contributing to their lives a certain peculiar buoyancy and peace. There is such a generic value in religion, which can not be attributed wholly to any of its component parts. But, like the intensity or extent of religion, this may manifest itself upon all levels of development. *Sound* piety, a tranquillity and happiness which mark the soul's real salvation, must be founded on truth, on an interpretation of life which expresses the fullest light. Again, then, we are referred to the test of truth for the fundamental justification of religion. There is a generic value which is deserving of the last word, but that word can be said only after a rigorous examination of the more fundamental values from which it is derived.

Religious truth is divisible into two judgments, involved in every religious belief, and answerable respectively to *ethical* and *cosmological* evidence. Since religion is a belief concerning the overruling control of human interests, it involves on the one hand a summing up of these interests, a conception of what the believer has at stake, in short, an ethical judgment; and on the other hand, an interpretation of the environment at large, in other words, a cosmological judgment. Religion construes the practical situation in its totality; which means that it generalizes concerning the content of fortune, or the good, and the sources of fortune, or nature. Both factors are invariably present, and no religion can escape criticism on this twofold ground.

The ethical implications of religion are peculiarly far-reaching, since they determine not only its conception of man, but also, in part, its conception of God. This is due to the fact that

JUSTIFICATION OF RELIGION

the term "God" signifies not the environment in its inherent nature, but the environment in its bearing on the worshipper's interests. It follows that whether God be construed as favorable or hostile will depend upon the worshipper's conception of these interests. Thus, for example, if worldly success or long life be regarded as the values most eagerly to be conserved, God must be feared as cruel or capricious; whereas, if the lesson of discipline and humility be conceived as the highest good, it may be reasonable to trust the providence of God without any change in its manifestation.

Furthermore, as we shall shortly have occasion to remark, it is characteristic of religion to insist, so far as possible, upon the favorableness of the environment. But this favorableness must be construed in terms of what are held to be man's highest interests. Consequently, the disposition and motive of God always reflect human purposes. This is the main source of the inevitable anthropomorphism of religion.

Conceptions of nature, on the other hand, define the degree to which the environment is morally determined, and the unity or plurality of its causes. Animism, for example, reflects the general opinion that the causes of natural events are wilful rather than mechanical. Such an opinion obtained at the time when no sharp distinction was made between inorganic and organic phenomena, the action of the environment being conceived as a play of impulses.

Religion is corrected, then, by light obtained from these sources: man's knowledge of his highest interests, and his knowledge of nature. As a rule, one or the other of these two methods of criticism tends to predominate, in accordance with the genius of the race or period. Thus, the evolution of Greek religion is determined mainly by the development of science. Xenophanes attacks the religion of his times on the ground of its crude anthropomorphism. "Mortals," he says, "think that the gods are born as they are, and have perception like theirs, and voice and form." But this naïve opinion Xenophanes corrects because it is not consistent with the new enlightenment concerning the ἀρχή, or first principle of nature. "And he [God] abideth ever in the same place, moving not at all; nor doth it befit him to go about, now hither, now thither."[5]

In a later age Lucretius criticised the whole system of Greek religion in terms of the atomistic and mechanical cosmology of Epicurus:

For verily not by design did the first-beginnings of things station themselves each in its right place guided by keen intelligence, nor did they bargain sooth to say what motions each should assume; but because many in number and shifting about in many ways throughout the universe they are driven and

JUSTIFICATION OF RELIGION

tormented by blows during infinite time past, after trying motions and unions of every kind at length they fall into arrangements such as those out of which this our sum of things has been formed.[6]

In the light of such principles Lucretius demonstrates the absurdity of hoping or fearing anything from a world beyond or a life to come. In this case, as in the case above, the religion of enlightenment does not differ essentially from the religion of the average man in its conception of the interests at stake, but only in its conception of the methods of worship or forms of imagery which it is reasonable to employ in view of the actual nature of the environment.

If, on the other hand, we turn to the early development of the Hebrew religion, we find that it is corrected to meet the demands not of cosmological but of ethical enlightenment. No question arises as to the existence or power of God, but only as to what he requires of those who serve him. The prophets represent the moral genius of the race, its acute discernment of the causes of social integrity or decay. "And when ye spread forth your hands, I will hide mine eyes from you: yea, when ye make many prayers, I will not hear: your hands are full of blood. Wash you, make you clean; put away the evil of your doings from before mine eyes; cease to do evil: learn to do well; seek judgment, relieve the oppressed, judge the fatherless, plead for the widow." [7]

But whichever of these two methods of criticism predominates, it is clear that they both draw upon bodies of truth which grow independently of religion. The history of Christianity affords a most remarkable record of the continual adjustment of religious belief to secular rationality. The offices of religion have availed no more to justify cruelty, intolerance, and bigotry than to establish the Ptolemaic astronomy or the Scriptural account of creation. This is more readily admitted in the case of natural science than in the case of ethics, but only because teachers of religion have commonly had a more expert acquaintance with moral matters than with the orbits of the planets or the natural history of the earth.

For the principles of conduct, like the principles of nature, must be derived from a study of the field to which they are applied. They require nothing more for their establishment than the analysis and generalization of the moral situation. If two or more persons conduct themselves with reference to one another and to an external object, their action either possesses or lacks, in some degree, that specific value which we call moral goodness. And by the principles of ethics we mean the principles which truly define and explicate this value. Now neither the truth nor

JUSTIFICATION OF RELIGION

the falsity of any religion affects these fundamental and essential conditions. If the teachings of religion be accepted as true, then certain factors may be added to the concrete practical situation; but if so, these fall within the field of morality and must be submitted to ethical principles. Thus, if there be a God whose personality permits of reciprocal social relations with man, then man ought, in the moral sense, to be prudent with reference to him, and may reasonably demand justice or good-will at his hands.

But the mere existence of a God, whatever be his nature, can neither invalidate nor establish the ethical principles of prudence, justice, and good-will. Were a God whose existence is proved, to recommend injustice, this would not affect in the slightest degree the moral obligation to be just. Moral revelation stands upon precisely the same footing as revelation in the sphere of theoretical truth: its acceptance can be justified only through its being confirmed by experience or reason. In other words, it is the office of revelation to reveal truth, but not to establish it. In consequence of this fact it may even be necessary that a man should redeem the truth in defiance of what he takes to be the disposition of God. Neither individual conscience nor the moral judgment of mankind can be superseded or modified save through a higher insight which these may themselves be brought to confirm. Whatever a man may think of God, if he continues to live in the midst of his fellows, he places himself within the jurisdiction of the laws which obtain there. Morality is the method of reconciling and fulfilling the interests of beings having the capacity to conduct themselves rationally, and ethics is the formulation of the general principles which underlie this method. The attempt to live rationally—and, humanly speaking, there is no alternative save the total abnegation of life—brings one within the jurisdiction of these principles, precisely as thinking brings one within the jurisdiction of the principles of logic, or as the moving of one's body brings one within the jurisdiction of the principles of mechanics.

Religion, then, mediates an enlightenment which it does not of itself originate. In religious belief the truth which is derived from a studious observation of nature and the cumulative experience of life, is heightened and vivified. Like all belief religion is conservative, and rightly so. But in the long run, steadily and inevitably, it responds to every forward step which man is enabled to take through the exercise of his natural cognitive powers. Only so does religion serve its real purpose of benefiting life by expanding its horizon and defining its course.

I have hitherto left out of account a certain

stress or insistence that must now be recognized as fundamental in religious development. This I shall call *the optimistic bias*. This bias is not accidental or arbitrary, but significant of the fact that religion, like morality, springs from the same motive as life itself, and makes towards the same goal of fruition and abundance. Life is essentially interest, and interest is essentially positive or provident; fear is incidental to hope, and hate to love. Man seeks to know the worst only in order that he may avoid or counterwork it in the furtherance of his interests. Religion is the result of man's search for support in the last extremity. This is true, even when men are largely preoccupied with the mere struggle for existence. It appears more and more plainly as life becomes aggressive, and is engaged in the constructive enterprise of civilization. Religion expresses man's highest hope of attainment, whether this be conceived as the efficacy of a fetich or the kingdom of God.

Such, then, are the general facts of religion, and the fundamental critical principles which justify and define its development. Religion is man's belief in salvation, his confident appeal to the overruling control of his ultimate fortunes. The reconstruction of religious belief is made necessary whenever it fails to express the last verified truth, cosmological or ethical. The direction of religious development is thus a resultant of two forces: the optimistic bias, or the saving hope of life; and rational criticism, or the progressive revelation of the principles which define life and its environment.

I shall proceed now to the consideration of types of religion which illustrate this critical reconstruction. The types which I shall select represent certain forms of inadequacy which I think it important to distinguish. They are only roughly historical, as is necessarily the case, since all religions represent different types in the various stages of their development, and in the different interpretations which are put on them in any given time by various classes of believers. I shall consider in turn, using the terms in a manner to be precisely indicated as we proceed, *superstition*, *tutelary religion*, and two forms of *philosophical religion*, the one *metaphysical idealism*, and the other *moral idealism*.

III

Superstition is distinguished by a lack of organization both in man and his environment. It is a direct cross-relationship between an elementary interest, passion, or need, and some isolated and capricious natural power. The deity is externally related to the worshipper, having private interests of his own which the worshipper respects only from motives of prudence. Religious observance takes the form of barter or propitiation —*do ut des, do ut abeas*. The method of superstition is arbitrary, furthermore, in that it is defined only by the liking or aversion of an unprincipled agency.

Let us consider briefly the type of superstition which is associated with the most primitive stage in the development of society.[8] The worshipper has neither raised nor answered the ethical question as to what is his greatest good. Indeed, he is much more concerned to meet the pressing needs of life than he is to co-ordinate them or understand to what they lead. He can not even be said to be actuated by the principle of rational self-interest. Like the brute, whose lot is similar to his own, he feels his wants severally, and is forced to meet them as they arise or be trampled under foot in the struggle for existence. There is little co-ordination of his interests beyond that which is provided for in the organic and social structure with which nature has endowed him. Over and above the instinct of self-preservation he recognizes in custom the principle of tribal or racial solidarity. But this is proof, not so much of a recognition of community of interest, as of the vagueness of his ideas concerning the boundaries of his own selfhood. The very fact that his interests are scattering and loosely knit prevents him from clearly distinguishing his own. He readily identifies himself not only with his body, but with his clothing, his habitation, and various trinkets which have been accidentally associated with his life. It is only natural that he should similarly identify himself with those other beings like himself with whom he is connected by the bonds of blood and of intimate contact. Morally, then, primitive man is an indefinite and incoherent aggregate of interests which have not yet assumed the form even of individual and community purpose.

To turn to the second, or cosmological, component, we find that primitive man's conception of ultimate powers is like his conception of his own interests in being both indefinite and incoherent. In consequence of the daily vicissitudes of his fortune, he is well aware that he is affected for better or for worse by agencies which fall outside the more familiar routine operations of society and nature. So great is the disproportion between the calculable and the incalculable elements of his life that he is like a man crouching in the dark, expecting a blow from any quarter. The agencies whose working can be discounted in advance form his secular world; but this world is narrow and meagre, and is overshadowed by a beyond which is both mysterious and terrible. Of the world beyond he has no single comprehensive idea, but he acknowledges it in his expectation of the injuries and benefits which he may at any time receive from it. It is an abyss whose depths he has never sounded, but which he is forced practically to recognize, since he is at the mercy of forces which emanate from it.

The method of primitive religion is the inevitable sequel. In behalf of the interests which represent him man must here, as ever, make the best terms he can with the powers which beset him. He has no concern with these powers except the desire to propitiate them. He has no knowledge of their working excepting as respects their bearing upon his interests. Obeying a law of human nature which is as valid now as then, he seeks for remedies whose proof is the cure which they effect. Let the association between a certain action on his own part and a favorable turn in the tide of fortune once be established, and the subsequent course of events will seem to confirm it. Coincidences are remembered and exceptions forgotten. Furthermore, his belief in the effectual working of the established plan is always justified by the difficulty of proving any other alternative plan to be better.

But, in order to understand superstition, it is not necessary to reconstruct the earliest period in the history of society, nor even to study contemporary savage life, for the superstitious intelligence and the superstitious method survive in every stage of development. They appear, for example, in mediæval Christianity; in Clovis's appeal to Christ on the battle-field: "Clotilda says that Thou art the Son of the living God, and that Thou dost give victory to those who put their trust in Thee. I have besought my gods, but they give me no aid. I see well that their strength is naught. I beseech Thee, and I will believe in Thee, only save me from the hands of mine enemies." The same period is represented by the petition attributed to St. Eloi, "Give, Lord, since we have given! *Da, Domine, quia dedimus!*"[9] In modern life the motive of superstition pervades almost all worship, appearing in sundry expectations of special favor to be gained by service or importunity.

The application of critical enlightenment to this type of religion has already been made with general consent. It is recognized that morally superstition represents the merely prudential level of life. It bespeaks a state of panic or a narrow regard for isolated needs and desires. Furthermore, it tends to emphasize these considerations and at the same time degrade the object of worship through claiming the attention of God in their behalf. The deity is conceived, not under the form of a broad and consecutive purpose, but under the form of a casual and desultory good-nature.

But superstition has been corrected mainly by the advancement of scientific knowledge. Science has pronounced finally against the belief in localized or isolated natural processes. Whether the mechanical theory be accepted or not, its method is beyond question, in so far as it defines laws and brings all events and phenomena under their control. In the dealings of nature there can be no favoritism, no special dispensations, no bargaining over the counter.

IV

The correction of superstition brings us to our second type, which I have chosen to call *tutelary religion*. It is distinguished by the fact that life is organized into a definite purpose, which, although still narrow and partisan with reference to humanity at large, nevertheless embraces and subordinates the manifold desires of a community. The deity represents this purpose in the cosmos at large, and rallies the forces of nature to its support. He is no longer capricious, but is possessed of a character defined by systematic devotion to an end. His ways are the ways of effectiveness. Furthermore, since his aims are identical with those of his worshippers, he is now loved and served for himself. It follows that he will demand of his followers only conformity to those rules which define the realization of the common aim, and that these rules will be enforced by the community as the conditions of its secular well-being. Ritual is no longer arbitrary, but is based on an enlightened knowledge of ways and means.

While this type of religion is clearly present in the most primitive tribal worship, it is best exemplified when a racial or national purpose manifests itself aggressively and self-consciously, as in the cases of ancient Assyria and Egypt. Here God is identified with the kingship, both being symbols of nationality. Among the Assyrians the national purpose was predominantly one of military aggrandizement. Istar communicates to Esar-haddon this promise of support: "Fear not, O Esar-haddon; the breath of inspiration which speaks to thee is spoken by me, and I conceal it not. . . . I am the mighty mistress, Istar of Arbela, who have put thine enemies to flight before thy feet. Where are the words which I speak unto thee, that thou hast not believed them? . . . I am Istar of Arbela; in front of thee and at thy side do I march. Fear not, thou art in the midst of those that can heal thee; I am in the midst of thy host." [10]

Egyptian nationality was identified rather with the principles of agriculture and political organization. The deity is the fertilizing Nile, or the judge of right conduct. There is recorded in

JUSTIFICATION OF RELIGION

the *Book of the Dead* the pleading of a soul before Osiris, in which the commands of the god are thus identified with the conditions of national welfare:

> I have not committed fraud and evil against men.
> I have not diverted justice in the judgment hall.
> I have not known meanness.
> I have not caused a man to do more than his day's work.
> I have not caused a slave to be ill treated by his overseer.
> I have not committed murder.
> I have not spoiled the bread of offering in the temple.
> I have not added to the weight of the balance.
> I have not taken milk from the mouths of children.
> I have not turned aside the water at the time of inundation.
> I have not cut off an arm of the river in its course.[11]

Similar illustrations might be drawn from the nationalistic phase of Hebraism. The same principle appears in mediæval Christianity, and is thus embodied in the prologue of the Salic Law, "Long live the Christ, who loves the Franks." In more recent times one might point to the Christianity of the Puritan revolution, not wholly misrepresented by the maxim popularly attributed to Cromwell, "Put your trust in God and keep your powder dry," or in Poor Richard's observation that "God helps them that help themselves."

Such is the religion of nationalism, sectarianism, of sustained but narrow purpose. I shall not attempt to formulate exhaustively the ideas through which this religion has been corrected. It is clear that its defect lies in its partisanship. All forms of partisanship yield slowly but inevitably to the higher conception of social solidarity. Such enlightenment reflects a recognition of community of interest, and a widening of sympathy through intercourse and acquaintance. Tutelary religion, in short, is corrected through the validity of the ethical principles of justice and good-will. The cosmological correction of this type of religion is due to the same enlightenment that discredits superstition, a knowledge, namely, of the systematic unity of the cosmos. The laws of nature are as indifferent to private purposes as they are to private desires, and whether these be personal or social in their scope. Furthermore, the universality of God is recognized in principle in the rules of worship. For a god of war or agriculture or politics can not be privately appropriated. If the observance of the principles proper to these institutions brings success to one, it brings success to all. In short, a god of nationality must be a god of all nations.

V

The correction of tutelary religion brings us at length to a type which may be said to be formally enlightened. Both components of belief, the ethical and the cosmological, are universalized. I shall call this type, in its general form, *philosophical religion*, since it recognizes the unities which systematic reflection defines. It recognizes, on the one hand, the summing up of life in a universal ideal, and on the other hand, a summing up of the total environment in some scientifically formulated generalization. It affirms the priority of justice and good-will over party interest, and the determination of the world without reference to special privilege. Religion is now the issue between the good—the highest good, the good of all—and the undivided cosmos.

Within the limits of philosophical religion thus broadly defined there is yet provision for almost endless variety of belief. Religions may still differ in tradition, symbolism, and ritual. They may differ as moral codes and sentiments differ, and reflect all shades of opinion as this is determined by discovery and criticism.

But I propose to confine myself to a difference which is at once the most broad and fundamental, and the most clearly defined in contemporary controversy. This difference relates to neither ethics nor cosmology exclusively, but to the religious judgment itself in which these two are united. How is the universe in its entirety to be construed with reference to the good? In both of the answers which I propose to consider it is claimed that goodness in some sense possesses the world. Hence both may be called *idealisms*. But in one of these answers, which I shall call *metaphysical idealism*, the cosmological motive receives the greater emphasis. The good is construed in terms of being; and, in order that it may be absolutely identified therewith, its original nature must, if necessary, be compromised. In the other, the *moral* motive predominates. It is held that goodness must not lose its meaning, even if it be necessary that its claims upon the cosmos should be somewhat abated.

Metaphysical idealism is the extreme form of the optimistic bias. It provides a moral individual with a sense of proprietorship in the universe; it justifies him in the belief that the moral victory has been won from all eternity. Goodness is held to be the very essence and condition of being.

Let me briefly state the inherent difficulty in this philosophy of religion. Being is judged to be identical with good. But the world of experience is not good; it must therefore be condemned as unreal. Of what, then, do goodness and being consist? If an empty formalism is

JUSTIFICATION OF RELIGION

to be avoided, the all-good-and-all-real must be restored to the world of experience. But as the all-real it can not consistently be identified with only a part of that world; and if it be identified with the whole, its all-goodness contradicts the moral distinction within the world of experience, between good and evil. The theory is now confronted with the opposite danger, that of materialism, or moral promiscuousness. Let me illustrate this full swing of the pendulum from formalism to materialism by briefly summarizing certain well-known types of religious philosophy.

At the formalistic extreme stands the Buddhistic *pessimism*,[12] which rests on a recognition of the inevitable taint of this world, of the implication of evil in life. To avoid this taint, the all-real-and-all-good must be freed even from existence. It can be conceived and attained only by denial. Nirvana is at once the all-real, the all-good, and—in terms of the existent world—nothing.

Other-worldliness is the Christian modification of the Oriental philosophy of illusion. Heaven is a world beyond, to be exchanged for this. It is not constituted by the denial of this world, as is Nirvana, but access to it is conditioned by such denial. It is goodness and happiness hypostasized, and offered as compensation for martyrdom. But since every natural impulse and source of satisfaction must be repudiated, it remains a purely formal conception, except in so far as the worldly imagination unlawfully prefigures it. Rigorously construed, it consists only in obedience, a willing of God's will, whatever that may be.

Mysticism,[13] which appears as a motive in all religions of this type, defines the all-real-and-all-good in terms of the consummation of a progression, certain intermediate stages of which constitute man's present activities. In Brahmanism, God is the perfect unity, which may be approximated by dwelling on identities and ignoring differences; in Platonism, God is the good-for-all, which may be approximated by dwelling exclusively upon the utilities and fitness of things. The absolute world still remains beyond this world and excludes it, although a hint of its actual nature may now be obtained. But there at once appears a formidable difficulty. So long as the absolute world is wholly separated from this world, and therefore purely formal, evil need not be imputed to it; but at the moment when it is conceived by completing and perfecting certain processes belonging to this world, it is committed to these processes with all their implications, and tends to be usurped by them. In other words, heaven, in so far as it obtains meaning, grows worldly.

In the conception which may be termed *pan-*

JUSTIFICATION OF RELIGION

logism, heaven is boldly removed to earth. It is identified with laws or other universals, that lie within the scope of human intelligence and control the course of nature. God is now immanent rather than transcendent; he has obtained a certain definable content. But the difficulty which has already appeared in mysticism now grows more formidable. How can it be said that a being that coincides with the known laws of nature works only good? Among the Stoics the attempt was made to conceive all necessities as somehow "beneficial," as somehow good in the commonly accepted sense of the term.[14] But even the Stoics found themselves compelled to abandon the common conception of goodness. And in Spinoza the motive of panlogism is clear and uncompromising.[15] God as the immanent order of the world is good only in that he is necessary—good only in so far as he satisfies the logical interest and enables the mind to understand. In panlogism, then, we find metaphysical idealism already compelled in behalf of its cardinal principle to deny the moral consciousness. But this is not all. For even were it to be admitted that mere system and order constitute the good, wholly without reference to their bearing on the concerns of life, the fact remains that even such a good does not fairly represent the character of this world. For experience conveys not only law, but also irrelevance and chaos; not only harmony but also discord.

To meet this last difficulty, and at the same time better to provide for the complexity of human interests, metaphysical idealism finally assumes the *æsthetic* form. The absolute world, the all-real-and-all-good, is boldly construed in terms of the historical process itself, with all its concreteness and immediacy. Endless detail, contrast, and even contradiction may be brought under the form of æsthetic value. The very flux of experience, the very struggles and defeats of life, are not without their picturesqueness and dramatic quality. Upon this romantic love of tumult and privation is founded the last of all metaphysical idealisms.[16] A strange sequel to the doctrine of despair with which our brief survey began!

I can only recapitulate most briefly the characteristic limitations of an æsthetic idealism. First, in spite of the fact that æsthetic value may be extraordinarily comprehensive in its content, as a value it is none the less narrow and exclusive. For in order that experience may have æsthetic value, an æsthetic interest must be taken in it. And even were all experience to satisfy some such interest, this would in no wise provide for the endless variety of non-æsthetic interests that are also taken in it. Thus, were it to be proved that life on the whole is picturesque, this

JUSTIFICATION OF RELIGION

would in no way affect the fact that it is also painful, stultifying, and otherwise abounding in evil.

But, even if it were to be granted that æsthetic value embraces and subordinates all other values, this higher value would still exist only where such an æsthetic interest was actually fulfilled. If it were assumed that the totality of the world is pleasing in the sight of God, this would in no way affect the fact that it is otherwise in the eyes of men. Those who furnish a spectacle which has dramatic value for an observer do not necessarily themselves share in that value. It is an incontrovertible fact that the æsthetic interests of men are actually defeated; and this whether or no some other æsthetic interest—that, for example, of a divine onlooker—is fulfilled.

But the radical defect of this æsthetic philosophy of religion lies in its absolute discrediting of moral distinctions. Optimism has so far overreached itself as to sacrifice the very meaning of goodness. In order that the ideal may possess the world, it has been reduced to the world. God is no more than a name for the unmitigated reality. Like Hardy's Spirit of the Years, he is the mere affirmation of things as they are:

> " I view, not urge; nor more than mark
> What designate your titles Good and Ill.
> 'Tis not in me to feel with, or against,
> These flesh-hinged mannikins Its hand upwinds

> To click-clack off Its preadjusted laws;
> But only through my centuries to behold
> Their aspects, and their movements, and their mould." [17]

Morally, there could be no more sinister interpretation of life. It offers itself as a philosophy of hope, promising the lover of good that his purpose shall be fulfilled, nay, that it is fulfilled from all eternity. But when the pledge is redeemed, it is found to stipulate that the good shall mean only life as it is already possessed. In other words, man is promised what he wants if he will agree to want what he has. This is worse than a sorry jest. It is a philosophy of moral dissolution, discrediting every downright judgment of good and evil, removing the grounds upon which is based every single-minded endeavor to purify and consummate life. John Davidson says: "Irony integrates good and evil, the constituents of the universe. It is that Beyond-Good-and-Evil which somebody clamoured for." [18] Irony is indeed the last refuge of that uncompromising optimism that equates goodness and being.

VI

But the bankruptcy of metaphysical idealism does not end the matter. There is another idealism in which religious faith both confirms moral endeavor and gives it the incentive of hope. This idealism establishes itself upon an unequivocal acceptance of moral truth. It calls good good and evil evil, with all the finality which attaches to the human experience of these things, leaving no room for compromise. Its faith lies in the expectation that the world shall become good through the elimination of evil; it manifests itself in the resolution to hasten that time. God is loved for the enemies he has made. Evil is hated without reservation as none of his doing, and man is free to reverence the Lord his God with all his heart.

From the stand-point of *moral idealism* the universe resumes something of its pristine ruggedness and grandeur. If, as James says, "the world appears as something more epic than dramatic," the dignity of life is enhanced and not diminished on that account.[19] Life is not a spiritual exercise the results of which are discounted in advance; but is actually creative, fashioning and perfecting a good that has never been. And the moment evil is conceived as the necessary but diminishing complement to partial success, the sting of it is gone. Evil as a temporary and accidental necessity is tolerable; but not so an evil which is absolutely necessary, and which must be construed with some hypothetical divine satisfaction.

This in no way contradicts the fact that the

fullest life under present conditions involves contact with evil. Innocence must be tragic if it is not to be weak. Jesus without the cross would possess something of that quality of unreality which attaches to Aristotle's high-minded man. But this does not prove that life involves evil; it proves only that life will be narrow and complacent when it is out of touch with things as they are. Since evil is now real, he who altogether escapes it is ignorant and idle, taking no hand in the real work to be done. Not to feel pain when pain abounds, not to bear some share of the burden, is indeed cause for shame. In that remarkable allegory, "The Man Who Was Thursday," Chesterton has most vividly presented this truth. In the last confrontation, the real anarchist, the spokesman of Satan, accuses the friends of order of being happy, of having been protected from suffering. But the philosopher, who has hitherto been unable to understand the despair to which he and his companions have been driven, repels this slander.

'I see everything,' he cried, 'everything that there is. Why does each thing on the earth war against each other thing? Why does each small thing in the world have to fight against the world itself? . . . So that each thing that obeys law may have the glory and isolation of the anarchist. So that each man fighting for order may be as brave and good a man as the dynamiter. So that the real lie of Satan may be

JUSTIFICATION OF RELIGION 251

flung back in the face of this blasphemer, so that by tears and torture we may earn the right to say to this man, "You lie!" No agonies can be too great to buy the right to say to this accuser, "We also have suffered."

'It is not true that we have never been broken. We have been broken upon the wheel. . . . We have descended into hell. We were complaining of unforgettable miseries even at the very moment when this man entered insolently to accuse us of happiness. I repel the slander; we have not been happy.' [20]

But the charge of happiness is to be repelled as a slander only because there are real sufferers in the world to make the charge. It is, after all, not happiness but insensibility which is the real disgrace. If the suffering is real, not to see it, not to feel it, not to heal it, is intolerable. To say, however, that suffering is wilfully caused in order that it may eventually contribute to an ultimate reconciliation, is to charge God with something worse than complacency. If life is a real tragedy it can be endured, and to enter into it will bring the deep satisfaction which every form of heroism affords. But if the tragedy of life be preconceived and wilfully perpetrated, it must be resented for the sake of self-respect. Even man possesses a dignity which is not consistent with puppetry and mock heroics.

Moral idealism means to interpret life consistently with ethical, scientific, and metaphysical truth. It endeavors to justify the maximum of hope, without compromising or confusing any enlightened judgment of truth. In this it is, I think, not only consistent with the spirit of a liberal and rational age, but also with the primary motive of religion. There can be no religion with reservations, fearful of increasing light. No man can do the work of religion without an open and candid mind as well as an indomitable purpose.

I can not here elaborate the evidence upon which moral idealism is grounded; but it might be broadly classified as ethical, cosmological, and historical. The ethical ground of moral idealism is the virtual unity of life, the working therein of one eventual purpose sustained by the goodwill of all moral beings. The cosmological proof lies in the moral fruitfulness and plasticity of nature. The historical proof lies in the fact of moral progress, in the advent and steady betterment of life.

VII

In conclusion I wish to revert to the topic of the generic proof of religion. We have defined the tests which any special religion must meet, and unless conformably to such tests it is possible to justify some form of idealism, it is clear that the full possibilities of religion as a source of strength and consolation must fail to be realized. But it may now be affirmed that there is a moral

JUSTIFICATION OF RELIGION

value in religion which is independent of the cosmological considerations which prove or disprove a special religion. No scientific or metaphysical evidence can controvert the fact that man is engaged in an enterprise which comprehends all the actualities and possibilities of life, and that the success of this enterprise is conditioned, in the end, on the compliance of the universe. A summing up of the situation as involving these two factors is morally inevitable. Some solution of the problem, assimilated and enacted, in other words, some form of piety, is no more than the last stage of moral growth.

The value of religious belief, in this generic moral sense, consists in the enlargement of the circle of life. Man knows the best and the worst; he walks in the open, apprehending the world in its full sweep and just proportions. An inclusive view of the universe, whatever it may reveal, throws into relief the lot of man. Religion promulgates the idea of life as a whole, and composes and proportions its activities with reference to their ultimate end. Religion advocates not the virtues in their severalty, but the whole moral enterprise. With this it affiliates all the sundry activities of life, thus bringing both action and thought under the form of service of the ideal. At the same time it offers a supreme object for the passions, which are otherwise divided against themselves, or vented upon unworthy and fantastical objects. Through being thus economized and guided, these moving energies may be brought to support moral endeavor and bear it with them in their current.

Piety carries with it also that sense of high resolve without which life must be haunted with a sense of ignominy. This is the immediate value of the good-will: the full deliverance of one's self to the cause of goodness. This value is independent of attainment. It is that *doing of one's best*, which is the least that one can do. Having sped one's action with good-will, one can only leave the outcome to the confluence and summing of like forces. But such service is blessed both in the eventualities and in a present harmony as well. The good of participation in the greatest and most worthy enterprise is proved in its lending fruitfulness, dignity, and momentousness to action; but also in its infusing the individual life with that ardor and tenderness which is called the love of humanity and of God, and which is the only form of happiness that fully measures up to the awakened moral consciousness.

Since religion emphasizes the unity of life and supplies it with meaning and dignity, it is the function of religion to kindle moral enthusiasm in society at large. Religion is responsible for the prestige of morality. As an institution, it is the appointed guardian and medium of that supreme value which is hidden from the world; of that finality which, in the course of human affairs, is so easily lost to view and so infrequently proved. It is therefore the function of the religious leader to make men lovers, not of the parts, but of the whole of goodness. Embarrassed by their very plenitude of life, men require to have the goodwill that is in them aroused and put in control. This, then, is the work of religion: to strike home to the moral nature itself, and to induce in men a keener and more vivid realization of their latent preference for the higher over the lower values. This office requires for its fulfilment a constructive moral imagination, a power to arouse and direct the contagious emotions, and the use of the means of personality and ritual for the creation of a sweetening and uplifting environment.

In culture and religion human life is brought to the elevation which is proper to it. They are both forms of discipline through which is inculcated that quality of magnanimity and service which is the mark of spiritual maturity. But while culture is essentially contemplative, farseeing, sensitive, and tolerant, religion is more stirring and vital. Both are love of perfection, but culture is admiration; religion, concern.

"Not he that saith Lord, Lord, but he that doeth the will of his Father, shall be saved." In religion the old note of fear is always present. It is a perpetual watchfulness lest the work of life be undone, or lest a chance for the best be forfeited.

NOTES

CHAPTER I

[1] Joseph Butler: *Sermon VII*, edited by Gladstone, p. 114. *Cf.* also *Sermon X*, on *Self-Deceit*.

[2] Nietsche: *Beyond Good and Evil*, translated by Helen Zimmern, p. 174.

[3] Edmund Burke: *A Vindication of Natural Society*, Preface, pp. 4, 5. (Boston, 1806.)

[4] The classic discussion of the whole matter is to be found in Aristotle's *Nicomachean Ethics*, Book I, Chapters I–VI, translated by J. E. C. Welldon. *Cf.* also Fr. Paulsen: *System of Ethics*, Book II, Chapters I, II, translated by Frank Thilly; G. H. Palmer: *The Nature of Goodness*, Chapters I, II; and W. James: *The Moral Philosopher and the Moral Life*, in his *Will to Believe*.

[5] The issue is presented clearly and briefly in Paulsen: *Op. cit.*, Book II, Chapter II, and in James's *Principles of Psychology*, Vol. II, pp. 549–559.

[6] Nietsche: *Op. cit.*, p. 107.

[7] Huxley: *Evolution and Ethics and Other Essays*, pp. 81–82. The first two essays contained in this volume, the *Prolegomena*, and the *Romanes Lecture*, contain a very interesting study of the relation of morality to nature.

[8] Huxley: *Op. cit.*, p. 13.

[9] G. K. Chesterton: *Napoleon of Notting Hill*, p. 291. The whole book is a brilliant satire, intended to show that all of the heroic sentiments and virtues depend on war and local pride.

[10] Nietsche: *Op. cit.*, pp. 59, 163, 176, 223, 235, 237, 122.

[11] Chesterton: *Heretics*, and *Orthodoxy*.

[12] Plato: *Protagoras*, p. 322 (marginal pagination), and *passim;* translated by Jowett.

NOTES

CHAPTER II

[1] Locke: *The Conduct of the Understanding*, Bohn's Library Edition, Vol. I, p. 72; also, *passim*.

[2] Locke: *Op. cit.*, p. 56.

[3] Descartes: *Discourse on Method*, translated by Veitch, pp. 13-14. Also, *passim*.

[4] Spinoza: *The Improvement of the Understanding*, translated by Elwes, Vol. II, p. 4.

[5] *Cf.* Plato's *Republic*, Books V-VII, *passim*.

[6] For further discussion of the meaning of duty, *cf.* Kant's *Critical Examination of the Practical Reason*, Book I, Chapter III, translated in Abbott's *Kant's Theory of Ethics*, p. 164; Bradley's *Ethical Studies*, Essays II and V; and Sidgwick's *Methods of Ethics*, Book I, Chapter III.

[7] Chesterton: *Napoleon of Notting Hill*, p. 162.

[8] G. E. Moore: *Principia Ethica*, Chapter III, Sect. 58-63.

[9] Locke: *Op. cit.*, p. 29.

[10] There is an excellent account of the questions that lie on the border between ethics and jurisprudence in S. E. Mezes's *Ethics, Descriptive and Explanatory*, Chapter XIII.

[11] Kant: *Fundamental Principles of the Metaphysic of Morals*, translated in Abbott's *Kant's Theory of Ethics*, p. 47.

[12] H. G. Lord: *The Abuse of Abstraction in Ethics*, in *Essays Philosophical and Psychological in Honor of William James*, pp. 376-377.

[13] John Davidson: *A Rosary*, pp. 77, 82.

[14] Maurice Maeterlinck: *The Measure of the Hours*, translated by A. T. de Mattos, p. 151. The essay in this volume, entitled "Our Anxious Morality," charges rationalism with destroying the romantic and mystical element in life.

CHAPTER III

[1] A good discussion of the several virtues will be found in Paulsen: *Op. cit.*, Book III.

[2] W. H. S. Jones: *Greek Morality*, p. 50.

[3] Jeremy Taylor: *Rules and Exercises of Holy Living*, edited by Ezra Abbot, p. 73.

[4] Jones: *Op. cit.*, p. 124.

NOTES

[5] Count Baldesar Castiglione: *The Book of the Courtier*, translated by Opdycke, p. 250.

[6] *Cf.* Hobbes: *Leviathan*, Chapters XIII, XIV, XV. In Hobbes's account, morality is reduced wholly to the prudential economy.

[7] H. G. Wells: *First and Last Things*, p. 82.

[8] Castiglione: *Op. cit.*, p. 257.

[9] Burke: *Op. cit.*, p. 8.

[10] Epictetus: *Discourses*, Book III, Chapter XXII, translated by Long, Vol. II, pp. 82, 83.

[11] Taylor: *Op. cit.*, p. 7.

[12] Epictetus: *Op. cit.*, Book II, Chapter XXI, translated by Long, Vol. I, p. 229.

[13] *Cf.* Hegel: *Philosophy of Right*, Third Part, Third Section, translated by S. W. Dyde; and *Philosophy of History*, Introduction, translated by J. Sibree.

[14] *Cf.* Plato's *Republic*, *passim*, but especially Book IV. Plato makes the state analogous to the individual organism, requiring baser classes that shall permanently supply its lower functions, as well as classes that shall supply its higher functions and so participate in its full benefits.

[15] Aristotle: *Politics*, Book II, Chapter V, translated by Jowett, p. 35. *Cf.* also Chapter II.

[16] Epictetus: *Op. cit.*, Book II, Chapter XV, translated by Long, Vol. I, p. 189.

[17] Sophocles: *Antigone*, translated by G. H. Palmer, pp. 61, 62.

[18] Munro and Sellery: *Medieval Civilization*, pp. 349-350.

[19] Castiglione: *Op. cit.*, p. 261.

[20] Quoted from Diog. Laert. by Jones, *op. cit.*, p. 69. For a full account, *cf.* Aristotle's *Nicomachean Ethics*, Books VIII and IX, translated by Welldon, pp. 245-314.

[21] Walter Bagehot: *Physics and Politics*, No. V, in the edition of the International Scientific Series, pp. 165-166. *Cf.* this chapter *passim*.

[22] Matthew Arnold: *Culture and Anarchy*, p. 100.

[23] Quoted by Jones: *Op. cit.*, p. 128.

[24] *Ibid.*

[25] Arnold: *Op. cit.*, pp. 25-26. *Cf. passim.*

[26] Euripides: *Medea*, translated by Gilbert Murray, pp. 67-68.

[27] *Cf.*, *e. g.*, Aristotle, *Nicomachean Ethics*, Book X. Also J. A. Farrer's *Paganism and Christianity*, *passim;* and Paulsen, *op. cit.*, Book I, Chapters I–III.

[28] Sir Thomas Browne: *Religio Medici*, edited by J. M. Dent & Co., p. 97.

[29] W. James: *Pragmatism*, p. 230.

[30] Browne: *Op. cit.*, pp. 118–119.

[31] *Ibid.*, p. 110.

[32] Castiglione: *Op. cit.*, pp. 304–305.

CHAPTER IV

[1] The nearest approach to such a philosophy of history is George Santayana's *Life of Reason*. The reader will find it the best book of reference for this and the following chapter. *Cf.* also, Samuel Alexander's *Moral Order and Progress*.

[2] Bagehot: *Op. cit.*, No. VI, pp. 208–209.

[3] *Ibid.*, p. 161.

[4] Nietsche: *Op. cit.*, pp. 65–66.

[5] For a general ethical discussion of the function of government, *cf.* Santayana: *Reason in Society*, Chapters III–VIII.

[6] Sophocles: *Antigone*, translated by Palmer, pp. 60, 63–64.

[7] I Samuel, Chapter VIII.

[8] Quoted in Taine's *Philosophy of Art in Greece*, translated by J. Durand, p. 130.

[9] Thucydides: *Peloponnesian War*, Book II, Chapters 37–40, translated by Jowett, pp. 117–119.

[10] Plato: *Republic*, Book IV, p. 433, translated by Jowett.

[11] Burke: *Op. cit.*, p. 45.

[12] For a brief statement of the elements of political science in their application to modern institutions, *cf.* E. Jenks: *A History of Politics*.

[13] Arnold: *The Future of Liberalism*, in the volume, *Mixed Essays, Irish Essays and Others*, p. 383. *Cf.* also the admirable essay on *Democracy* in the same volume.

[14] Plato: *Republic*, Book I, p. 335, translated by Jowett.

[15] Wells: *Op. cit.*, pp. 130–131.

CHAPTER V

[1] A good account of the meaning of art is to be found in Santayana's *Reason in Art*, Chapters I–III.

[2] For this whole topic of the æsthetic interest, *cf.* H. R. Marshall's *Pleasure, Pain, and Æsthetics*.

[3] For an interpretation of painting in terms of the perceptual process, *cf.* B. Berenson's *Florentine Painters of the Renaissance*, pp. 1–16; and *North Italian Painters of the Renaissance*, pp. 145–157.

[4] The best account of the emotions and instincts is to be found in James's *Principles of Psychology*, Vol. II, Chapters XXIV, XXV.

[5] Walter Pater: *The Renaissance*, p. 140.

[6] Taine: *Op. cit.*, pp. 112, 114–115, and *passim*.

[7] Pater: *Op. cit.*, pp. 129–130; *cf.* the chapter on *Leonardo da Vinci*, entire.

[8] Plato: *Republic*, Book III, p. 398, translated by Jowett. The whole of Books III and X are interesting in this connection.

[9] In connection with the general topic of the moral criticism of art, *cf.* Santayana's *Reason in Art*, Chapters IX–XI; also Ruskin's *Lectures on Art*, Lectures II–IV.

[10] Aristotle: *Nicomachean Ethics*, Book X.

[11] *Cf.* the *Republic*, Book X.

[12] Arthur Benson: *Beside Still Waters*, pp. 138–139. *Cf.* also pp. 143–144.

[13] Pater: *Op. cit.*, pp. 249, 250; *cf.* the *Conclusion, passim*.

[14] James: *Op. cit.*, Vol. I, pp. 125–126.

[15] *Republic;* Book X, p. 606, translated by Jowett.

[16] *Ibid.*, Book III, p. 399.

[17] Aristotle: *Politics*, Book VIII, Chapter V, translated by Jowett, p. 252.

[18] Taine: *The Ideal in Art*, translated by J. Durand, pp. 42 *sq.*

[19] Tolstóy: *What is Art?* X, translated by Leo Wiener, p. 227.

[20] Arnold: *Culture and Anarchy*, pp. 37, 38. *Cf.* Chapter I, *passim*.

[21] *Republic*, Book III, p. 401, translation by Jowett.

CHAPTER VI

[1] This chapter is reprinted from the *Harvard Theological Review* for April, 1909.

[2] I have treated this matter more fully in my *Approach to Philosophy*, Chapters III and IV. At the close of that book the reader will find a selected bibliography of the subject.

[3] John Henry Newman: *Apologia pro Vita Sua*, p. 239. The whole book is of interest in this connection.

[4] Munro and Sellery: *Mediæval Civilization*, p. 69.

[5] *Fragments of Xenophanes*, in Burnet's *Early Greek Philosophy*, p. 115.

[6] Lucretius: *De Rerum Natura*, Book I, lines 1021–1028, translated by Munro.

[7] *Isaiah* 1:15–17.

[8] For a brief account of primitive religion, *cf.* J. B. Pratt's *Psychology of Religious Belief*. For a fuller account, *cf.* F. B. Jevons's *Introduction to the History of Religion*.

[9] Munro and Sellery: *Op. cit.*, pp. 80, 75.

[10] A. H. Sayce: *Babylonians and Assyrians*, p. 253.

[11] A. Wiedemann: *Religion of the Ancient Egyptians*, p. 250.

[12] *Cf.* H. C. Warren's *Buddhism in Translation*.

[13] The reader will find a good exposition of mysticism in Royce's *World and the Individual*, First Series, Lectures II, IV, V.

[14] *Cf.*, *e. g.*, Epictetus: *Discourses*, Book II, Chapter VIII.

[15] *Cf.* Spinoza's *Ethics*, *passim*, translated by Elwes.

[16] *Cf.* Royce's account of Romanticism and Hegel, in his *Spirit of Modern Philosophy*, Lectures VI, VII. This motive, together with the motive of mysticism, appears in such writings as J. McT. E. McTaggart's *Studies in Hegelian Cosmology*, Chapter IX; and A. E. Taylor's *Problem of Conduct*, Chapter VIII.

[17] Thomas Hardy: *The Dynasts*, Part I, p. 5.

[18] John Davidson: *A Rosary*, p. 88.

[19] James: *Pragmatism*, p. 144. The whole chapter is a brilliant representation of the stand-point of moral idealism.

[20] G. K. Chesterton: *The Man Who Was Thursday*, pp. 278–279.

INDEX

ACHIEVEMENT, 79, 81, 97.
Adaptation, 22.
Æsthetic Interest, definition of, 179; varieties of, 181 *ff.*, 189; moral limitation of, 190; self-sufficiency of, 192; exaggeration of, 192, 195, 198 *ff.*; its pervasiveness, 194 *ff.*; vicariousness of, 197; stimulating character of, 201, 203 *ff*; liberality of, 209 *ff.*; in religion, 246 *ff.*
Aimlessness, 94.
Anarchism, 107.
Aristotle, quoted, 100, 106, 192, 204.
Arnold, M., quoted, 108, 109, 112, 164, 211.
Art, moral criticism of, Ch. V; its liability to moral criticism, 173 *ff.*; definition of, 177; distinction between industrial and fine, 177 *ff.*; emotion in, 182 *ff.*; representative function of, 185 *ff.*, 203 *ff.*; Greek, 185 *ff.*; of Renaissance, 187; censorship of, 190; stimulating character of, 201 *ff.*; truth in, 205 *ff.*; universality and particularity of, 207 *ff.*; and liberality, 209 *ff.*; moral function of, 212.
Asceticism, 79, 81, 92 *ff.*

BAGEHOT, quoted, 106, 127, 132.
Beauty, and goodness, 172 *ff.*
Belief, and religion, 216, 220, 228.
Benson, A., quoted, 194.
Bigotry, 79, 81, 101 *ff.*
Browne, Sir Thomas, quoted, 115, 117, 118.
Buddhism, 243.
Burke, quoted, 6, 92, 158, 214.
Butler, J., quoted, 1.

CASTIGLIONE, quoted, 89, 90, 119.
Character, 97.
Chesterton, G. K., 32; quoted, 28, 55, 250.
Christianity, 94, 111, 114 *ff.*, 140, 158, 187, 228, 239, 243.
Civilization, 3, 6, 10, 23, 32, 124, 137, 167, 170, 215. See Progress.
Competition, 14, 129, 130; relation to morality, 24 *ff.*
Conscience, 34, 36. See Duty.
Conservatism, 144 *ff.*
Convention, 36, 38 *ff.*
Cosmological, test of religion, 224, 225, 234, 237, 240, 241, 252.
Courage, 95.
Culture, 211, 255. Chap. V, *passim.*

263

INDEX

Cynics, the Greek, 92 *ff.*, 137.

DAVIDSON, J., quoted, 70, 248.
Democracy, 29, 39; modern idea of, 158 *ff.*, 163 *ff.*
Descartes, quoted, 35.
Desire, 11. See Interest.
Discussion, 106, 132.
Dogmatism, 4.
Duty, Ch. II, 40, 72; formalism and, 76.

EGOISM, theoretical, 59 *ff.*; practical, 79, 81, 101.
Emotion, and art, 182 *ff.*, 201 *ff.*
Epictetus, quoted, 93, 96, 100.
Equality, 65, 66, 158 *ff.*, 163 *ff.*
Ethics, and history, 124; and religion, 224 *ff.*, 233, 240, 241, 252; independence of, 228. See Morality.
Euripides, quoted, 114.
Evil, 11, 15, 84, 86; religious conception of, 243 *ff.* 249 *ff.* See Good, Vice, Formalism, Materialism.

FAITH, 33, 71.
Fine Art. See Art.
Formalism, 74 *ff.*, 92; and duty, 76, 77; varieties of, 79, 81, 92, 98, 107, 116, 209, 242.
Freedom, 36, 107, 164.

GOD, 216, 224 *ff.*, 229, 232, 237, 240, 245, 249.
Good, basal definition of, 11 *ff.*, 44; definition of moral, 15 *ff.*; relativity of, 45 *ff.*; relation to beautiful, 172 *ff.*, 212.

Good-will, logic of, 67 *ff.*; virtue of, 79, 81, 113 *ff.*, 158.
Government, 14; progress in, 148 *ff.*; Platonic theory of, 148; definition of, 150; ancient forms of, 152 *ff.*; summary of modern, 160 *ff.*
Greece, morality of, 110, 114; government in, 154 *ff.*; art of, 185 *ff.*, 204; religion of, 226.

HAPPINESS, 18, 115, 116 *ff.*
Hardy, T., quoted, 247.
Health, 79, 81, 88 *ff.*
Hebrews, government of, 152; religion of, 227, 239.
Hedonism, 16.
History, meaning of, 123 *ff.*
Hobbes, 89.
Honesty, 88.
Huxley, theory of morality and nature, 21 *ff.*

IDEALISM, metaphysical, 242 *ff.*; æsthetic, 246; moral 248 *ff.*
Idleness, 94.
Imagination, 28, 69, 111.
Imprudence, 79, 81, 85 *ff.*
Incapacity, 79, 81, 83.
Individualism, 34 *ff.*
Injustice, 79, 81, 103. See Justice.
Institutions, their necessity, 3, 147. See Government.
Intelligence, 79, 81, 82 *ff.*
Interest, definition of, 11, 43; organization of, 13, 14, 19; variety of, 16, 17; the

higher, 52; conflict of, 53; objective validity of, 54; private, 57 *ff*.; the potential, 67, 68, 167; present and ulterior, 74 *ff*.; economies of, 78; simple, 78, 81, 82 *ff*.; reciprocity of, 78, 81, 87 *ff*.; incorporation of, 78, 81, 95 *ff*.; fraternity of, 78, 81, 105 *ff*.; universal system of, 79, 81, 112 *ff*.; and progress, 132; and reform, 137; and revolution, 139; and government, 148 *ff*.; the æsthetic, 179; the theoretical, 180, 193; varieties of the æsthetic, 181 *ff*. See Æsthetic Interest.

JAMES, W., quoted, 116, 199, 249.
Justice, meanings of, 63, 79, 81, 105, 158, 163; logic of, 63 *ff*.

KANT, quoted, 64.

LAISSEZ-FAIRE, 108.
Liberality, 156; and art, 209.
Life, morality as the organization of, Ch. I; versus mechanism, 10, 22; morality one with, 19, 27; method of, 23.
Locke, quoted, 34, 35, 62.
Logic, of the moral appeal, Ch. II; and the imagination, 69.
Lord, H. G., quoted, 69.
Lucretius, quoted, 226.

MAETERLINCK, quoted, 71.
Manners, 121.
Materialism, 74 *ff*., 84; varieties of, 79, 81, 94, 101, 110, 243.
Mechanical Nature, 12; lack of value in, 9, 84; and progress, 130.
Menander, quoted, 88.
Metaphysics and religion, 242 *ff*.
Moderation, 87.
Moore, G. E., critique of egoism, 59 *ff*.
Morality, as the organization of life, Ch. I; the dulness of, 1; as verified truth, 7; its universal pertinence, 7 *ff*.; essential to life, 9, 32; natural genesis of, 9 *ff*.; basal definition of, 13; and nature, 20 *ff*.; and competition, 24 *ff*.; the logic of, Ch. II; rational ground of, 38, 40 *ff*.; material and formal aspects of, 74 *ff*., 121; and progress, Ch. IV; and art, Ch. V; and æsthetic standards, 172 *ff*.; and religion, Ch. VI; and idealism, 248 *ff*.
Mysticism, 116, 244; and art, 208.

NATIONALISM, 99.
Nature, genesis of morality in, 9 *ff*.; and morality, 20 *ff*.; theories of, in religion, 224, 225, 234, 237, 240.
Newman, J. H., quoted, 220.

Nietsche, his conception of morality, 1, 5, 6, 20, 29 *ff.*, 165.

OPTIMISM, 230, 242, 247.
Other-worldliness, 115, 243.
Overindulgence, 79, 81, 84 *ff.*

PANLOGISM, 244.
Pater, quoted, 185, 188; on the æsthetic interest, 196.
Patience, 95.
Pessimism, 114, 243.
Philosophy, of history, 123 *ff.*; and religion, 241 *ff.*
Piety, 67, 68, 120, 223, 253, 254.
Pity, 111, 163.
Plato, quoted, 32; individualism in, 37; nationalism in, 100; account of disinterested activity in, 135 *ff.*; theory of government in, 148; on art, 190, 193, 202, 212; on religion, 244.
Pleasure, its relation to morality, 16 *ff.*
Preference, 50; the quantitative principle of, 55 *ff.*, 127.
Progress, moral test of, Ch. IV, 127; definition of, 125 *ff.*; principles of, 130 *ff.*; by constructive reform, 134 *ff.*; by revolution, 139 *ff.*
Prudence, 79, 81, logical ground of, 43 *ff.*; limits of, 49, 88, 90, 91, 94; meaning of, 87 *ff.*; basal character of, 91; in religion, 232.
Purpose, logic of, 50 *ff.*; virtue of, 95 *ff.*

RADICALISM, 145 *ff.*
Rationality, 37, 42, 65; and progress, 134, 142; in government, 152.
Reform, 134 *ff.*
Religion, 79, 81; and good-will, 113; mysticism in, 117; as an institution, 148; and progress, 170; moral justification of, Ch. VI; moral necessity of, 214 *ff.*; definition of, 215 *ff.*; quantitative tests of, 218 *ff.*; psychological study of, 220; belief in, 216, 220; therapeutic test of, 222 *ff.*; superstitious, 232 *ff.*; primitive, 233 *ff.*; and ethics, 224 *ff.*, 233, 240, 241, 252; cosmological test of, 224, 225, 234, 237, 240, 241, 252; tutelary, 237 *ff.*; Assyrian, 238; Egyptian, 238; Hebrew, 227, 239; philosophical, 241 *ff.*; generic proof of, 252 *ff.* See Piety, Good-will, Worship and Christianity.
Revolution, definition of, 139; the Christian, 140; the French, 141.
Rightness, 18. See Virtue.

SATISFACTION, 11, 79, 81, 83.
Scepticism, 4 *ff.*, 36, 108.
Sentimentalism, 98 *ff.*, and art, 209.
Society, Chap. I, *passim*, 38; prudential basis of, 89; character of modern, 39, 166; progress in, 126, 132; con-

tinuity of, 143; and the æsthetic interest, 195, 211.
Sophocles, quoted, 102, 151.
Sordidness, 79, 81, 94.
Spinoza, quoted, 35.
Stoics, religion of, 245. See Epictetus.
Struggle for existence, 30; its relation to morality, 21 *ff.*; its relation to progress, 130.
Superstition, 232 *ff.*
Survival, 24, 131.

TACT, 88.
Taine, quoted, 185.
Taylor, J., quoted, 86, 94.
Temperance, 90.
Thrift, 68, 87.
Thucydides, quoted, 156.
Tolerance, 38, 105, 164.
Tolstóy, on art, 207.
Truth, of art, 205 *ff.*; of religion, 220 *ff.*
Truthfulness, 96. See Veracity.

Tyranny, 36, 39, 151 *ff.*

VALUE, the simpler terms of, 11, 82; definition of moral, 15; varieties of moral, 79, 81.
Veracity, 88, 96, 105.
Vice, varieties of, 79, 81. See Virtue, Formalism, and Materialism.
Virtue, the order of, Ch. III; verification of, 73; varieties of, 73, 79; classification of, 73 *ff.*; table of, 81. See under particular virtues, Prudence, etc.

WAR, and morality, 24 *ff.*, 30; the passing of, 28, 162; and progress, 131.
Wells, H. G., quoted, 89, 167.
Worldliness, 79, 81, 110 *ff.*
Worship, 122, 232, 235, 237, 240.

XENOPHANES, quoted, 226.

THE APPROACH TO PHILOSOPHY

BY

RALPH BARTON PERRY

12mo. Net $1.50

"One closes the book with the conviction of having enjoyed and profited by a gracefully written, a skilfully planned, and a well sustained discussion of the vital relationship to practical interests."
—*Philosophical Review.*

"Dr. Perry possesses the power of writing English that is lucid and distinguished."—*(London) Spectator.*

"Dr. Perry does not introduce us to philosophy by making his volume a mere history or a mere exposition of systems. It has a life and vigor of its own."
—*Mind.*

CHARLES SCRIBNER'S SONS